Lyntie

The Bravehound golden retriever dog who helped

me live with my grief and military PTSD.

By C.G. Buswell

Also by C.G. Buswell

Novels

The Grey Lady Ghost of the Cambridge Military Hospital: Grey and Scarlet 1

The Drummer Boy: Grey and Scarlet 2

Buried in Grief

One Last War

Group

The Fence

Zombie Haven

Short Stories

Christmas at Erskine

Halloween Treat

Angelic Gift

Burnt Vengeance

The Release

Christmas Presence

Torturous Grief

Operation Wrath

For Bernard, Christopher, and Bernadette who donated and named Lynne to Bravehound in memory of their dear wife and mother, and to Fiona for having the incredible idea of setting up the remarkable charity, and to all who have worked with her to the benefit of veterans like me who can live with such debilitating conditions because of our loving dogs. My grateful thanks.

FOREWORD

There is a 15th Century Japanese art form called Kintsugi. It means to "Join with gold" and is used for repairing broken pottery in a way that does not try to disguise cracks and breakages, but instead brings the pot or vase together again, in a changed way, making the flaws and cracks as beautiful and positive as they can be.

Getting to know the veterans who come to Scottish military charity BRAVEHOUND for support is a huge privilege.

All of us face difficulties in our lives but it is incredibly moving, humbling and inspirational to read about the tragic loss experienced by Chris Buswell and his wife Karla coupled with the effects of Post Traumatic Stress Disorder related to his military service, the invisible wounds of war.

At BRAVEHOUND we are proud to have partnered Chris with one of our assistance dogs, BRAVEHOUND Lynne.

Golden retriever BRAVEHOUND Lynne brings comfort and companionship to this incredibly talented writer and his family, "joining them with gold" and we are so proud of them all and to be part of this, their story.

Fiona MacDonald Founder and Director of BRAVEHOUND.

CONTENTS

Hope   1

Help   4

General Practitioner   8

The Police   10

SSAFA   14

Signs of Suicide   17

The Funeral   20

Combat Stress   23

Soundproofing   27

Earplugs   30

Medicines   32

Noisc-Cancelling Headphones   35

Sleep   39

Counselling   43

Cruse Bereavement Care   47

Psychology   49

Eye Movement Desensitisation and Reprocessing   54

Holidays   57

The Compassionate Friends   68

Say Their Name   71

Photographs   74

Bravehound   76

Triggers   88

Anger   95

Denial   101

Flashbacks   103

Anxiety   106

Depression   109

Seasonal Affective Disorder   111

Feeling of Dread   117

Paranoia   119

Sweating and Going Thermonuclear   121

Low Concentration   123

What If…   125

Answers   128

Imposter Syndrome   131

Survivor's Guilt   135

Being Hyper   138

Shedding Excess Baggage   140

Learning to Say No   142

PTSD Resolution   144

Hypnotherapy   146

Mindfulness   148

Childhood   150

Marriage and Relationships   155

Diet   159

Psychic Mediums   164

Seeing and Talking   168

to the Dead   168

Illegal Drugs,   171

Alcohol and Smoking   171

Humour in Grief and PTSD   175

At Least   179

Driving   181

Short-Term Goals   183

Fireworks   186

Mediation   188

A Fresh Start   189

Daily treat   191

Be Grateful for Something Each Day   193

Exercise   195

Walking   197

Pets   199

Burp Burps!   201

Lockdown   203

Christmas, Birthdays   207

and Anniversaries   207

Still Learning/Ruminating   209

My Future   212

Your future   215

Acknowledgements   217

Other books I've written: 219

CHAPTER 1:

HOPE

I'm standing on the edge of a cliff. My son, Angus, has taken his life. He was the victim of a heinous crime one year earlier. The police failed to remove a torn first draft of his suicide letter to his friends from his flat, urging them not to tell us what happened to him. He wanted to spare us from knowing what he'd bravely lived with for one year. I can't cope with the gut-wrenching, heart-tearing emotional anguish that courses through my body. It is an unwelcome guest. All I want is for my son to be alive once more. My toes are over the damp earth and bracken. I hope that the drop and landing on the jagged rocks far below will be enough to end my suffering.

I've developed Post Traumatic Stress Disorder from my time as an army nurse. I no longer want to see the bodies that I've cared for in life, and then death. I know they aren't there. I helped put them in the mortuary fridges or performed last offices and wrapped them in a shroud or sheets. Yet they are as real as if I have been transported back in time. I don't understand what my mind is putting me through. I need it to end. I feel in my pocket for the codeine and paracetamol combination tablets I've stockpiled for my knee and lower legs' pains. If I don't have the resolve to step off, I'll be going to my favourite spot, a place nearby that my previous faithful dog, Bessie, and I would go for peace, especially on mornings when I'd seen the helmeted and visored pilot standing at the foot of my bed. He visits, along with the navigator, on the anniversary of the fatal Tornado jet crash in Cyprus, or whenever the news that day had been about a plane crash somewhere. But now they visit throughout the day and night.

I no longer have my sweet Bess to comfort me. I had the tough decision three years previously to put her to sleep, to end her painful suffering at fourteen years. I long for her companionship, for her to be by my side as I try to balance working on my failing businesses whilst juggling doing the housework and caring for my disabled wife, Karla. Not even the thought of my beautiful daughter, Abigail, can stop me swallowing a fatal overdose or stepping off into the sweet release of oblivion. My jacket is weighed down by stones for the approaching tide to sweep my body from the rocks and down into the depths of the North Sea. I've a can of Irn-Bru in my hand. One last favourite drink, along with a hip flask of my favourite malt whisky. All to wash down strip after strip of codeine and paracetamol tablets.

My parents no longer talk to me, all because I did not want the alleged paedophile family member attending my son's funeral. I have no support. I'm kept too busy supporting my wife and daughter, financially, emotionally, and physically, to care about myself.

Noises from an unknown source are keeping me awake throughout the night, and they happen during the day. The council and police are doing nothing to stop the suspected person from making the deliberate noises. They set off a chain of thought and visions in my head. The noises sound like the explosion the aircraft made when it crashed. I relive hearing it and being scrambled to the helipad and the awful things I saw and had to do. I relive carrying bodies from the helicopter, awash with blood and sea water, and into the ambulance. I'm back in the ambulance, covered in strangers' blood, shut in with two corpses, blood dripping from the stretchers, from the piercing wounds of parts of the aircraft. I'm finally stepping down the ambulance steps, carrying two heavy bodies into the mortuary and am reliving processing them. I need these visions to stop. I need the other bodies to stop appearing. I've seen a lot of death in my nursing career, and now I'm reliving them, when all I want is to see the body of my son, to restart his heart and lungs, like I've done many times for other people. Life seems so unfair, and I need mine to end.

I sway over the edge, looking at the drop for one last time. I can't see the beauty of the Aberdeenshire coast anymore. Life seems so grey. I don't see the gentle lapping of the water over the rocks, nor the ebb as it washes away. I can't hear the gentle calls of the gulls and the oystercatchers. Nor do I see the vibrant colours of the hills and heather or the pretty cloud formations forming patterns in the sky above. I don't even see the majestic reassuring beauty of the nearby lighthouse which dominates the skyline.

But I can hear the distant sound of a barking dog and my mind switches back to the military charity that my kind General Practitioner referred me to. A charity run by a benevolent lady who would turn into my earthbound guardian angel. A charity called Bravehound, who had assessed me as needing a PTSD assistance dog. A dog that I was assured would change my life. I step back from the edge, open my can, swallow two painkillers, and start the long walk home, dropping stones from my pocket as I go. One day I will have a dog bounding over the heather nearby or trotting by my side. A faithful companion once more. A friend to steer me through life.

Hope, there is always hope, dear reader.

CHAPTER 2:

HELP

Losing a child is catastrophic. Like me, others can learn to live with their loss, given time, with lots of help. The same is true for those fellow military veterans who are living with PTSD. Our lives become a new sort of normal. A normal we don't want but must become resilient to. I learnt early on both journeys that I couldn't do it alone. I tried. But I burnt myself out.

If you are reading this book because you fall into either category, I will speak to you directly. Learn from the heavy footsteps I trod on these paths. Accept help from wherever and whenever it is offered. I hope this book helps guide you. I've intentionally kept the chapters short. Grief and PTSD will mess with your brain and your attention span may have become narrowed. This is part of the new normal. It's been seven years since Angus took his life and I developed PTSD. I never thought I would get through seven minutes, from the time the police knocked on our door in the middle of the night to tell Karla and me that Angus was dead, by his own hands. Yet, seven years later, we are all here. We got through seven minutes, seven hours, then seven days, weeks, and then months. Each of us, including our beloved daughter Abigail, has had our crises, and with the help of others, has survived. And thrived. We each enjoy life once more.

Abigail is on her way to be a highly qualified counsellor, specialising in grief. Karla enjoys the company of a wide circle of friends and takes pleasure in her crafts, especially card-making and scrapbooking. I have my dear Lynne, my saviour, by my side throughout the day and night. Ready to give me doggie cuddles on command. She has been a blessing to all three of us. I've put fingers on keyboards and have written several books.

One day, you will find pleasure in life again. Read this book at your own pace. Dip in and out of certain chapters or jump ahead to those that matter to you. Or even flick through to the end of each chapter where I give you a sentence of my thoughts to follow.

Above all, talk to your friends and family. Shrug off your pride and accept the kindness of strangers. This will be difficult. It was for me. My military background taught me to be resourceful, resilient, and to problem solve. I'd forgotten about teamwork, though. Turn to the resources that I describe further in this book, accept help from military and bereavement charities, let them become your new team. That is why they are there. Fundraisers and donators want you to have the help available. One day, you might donate financially, or with your time. But you need to be in that better place first. That's why I donate the profits of my writing back to the charities that helped my wife, daughter and myself get back on our feet. They embraced us in a cocoon of care while we worked through our trauma and learnt coping mechanisms.

I won't give you much homework. But I would like you to put this book down, after you've read this paragraph, and take a few deep breaths in through your nostrils and slowly exhale through your mouth. Slow your breathing down and feel your heartbeats slow too. Then take some time acknowledging your loss, or your new medical condition.

Welcome back. Now let's get you back on your feet and off your bootstraps. Let's give you hope and the tools to get on with this gift of life.

The first thing I'd like you to do, now that you've acknowledged your grief and condition, is to share your feelings and worries with your loved ones, be that family or friends. Don't hold back. If they don't want to listen, then they aren't really your friends, are they? But those that do; cherish and keep them close. They won't mind if you talk about the same things over and over, they care and want you to heal. And you will.

The second thing I'd like you to do is phone your GP surgery and make an appointment to see your doctor. You may need to see several doctors before you find the one who understands you as an individual and not just a prescription. Though tablets are important, and I'll talk about them later. Like many veterans with PTSD, I only saw an understanding doctor after getting into trouble with the police. I'm not ashamed. Someone was banging a ladder outside my daughter's bedroom window and rattling railings on the morning of my son's funeral for over two hours, without the police stopping the person, despite several calls to them from all three of us. In the heat of the moment, I challenged the person. I'm just glad that railings stopped me from going close to the person. Yes, I was most definitely showing abusive and threatening behaviour in the CCTV cameras aimed at my door. I'm also glad that the court system saw my need for professional care and referred me to Combat Stress and, finally, I saw a caring doctor. I hope your route to care will be less challenging and emotional. Make that appointment now.

I'd seen several doctors previously, but each were locums and told me my problem was social and to go away. The doctor I now see is lovely. She has an interest in mental health and quickly diagnosed me with PTSD and set me on a path to recovery which involved a grief counsellor who, after about eight sessions, realised that I needed more specialised care and told me about a lady who performed Eye Movement Desensitisation and Reprocessing with the local emergency services, a clinical procedure that I'd never heard of, but will talk about later. Sadly, I couldn't afford these fees. My businesses had collapsed, and we were running out of savings. But, after talking this through with my GP, who had insisted that I attend regular appointments with her, she referred me to the local National Health Service Psychiatric Hospital, the Royal Cornhill in Aberdeen. But I would be expected to wait months for an appointment. This was eventually a nine month wait. But more about this later. I'm giving you food for thought.

Whether you are former military, or civilian, there are many organisations and charities that will help you. Please also note that the shock of seeing your loved one dead can also cause PTSD and you will need specialised treatment, especially if you found your loved one. This will help you live your new normal life. I won't say recover, nor move on. You can't do either after losing a loved one, especially a child. You slowly rebuild your life and learn to find enjoyment again. I'll go through the various charities and organisations that helped my family and me.

For the moment, I want you to accept that you will need the kindness of strangers and accept the help offered to you.

CHAPTER 3:

GENERAL PRACTITIONER

You have made that appointment, haven't you?

Thanks, that's great! Your doctor is your first route to specialised care. The surgery is a font of local knowledge and can direct you to free grief counselling from several charitable sources. These will be highly trained practitioners who will embrace you in care and help unravel your thoughts and emotions and then guide you to put them back into their correct slots, like a filing cabinet in your mind. I'll talk more about these later and who helped my family and me.

Your doctor can also refer you to other specialists within the National Health Service. Get that referral in quick, because there will be a wait, but when you are in the system, boy, do you get cared for. Don't neglect any part of your health. Your family and friends need you and you'll need to be in top condition to wrestle with grief.

What I love about my GP is that she really listens. She forgets about the time. No clocks are looked at. She turns away from her monitor and keyboard. The prescription pad is well away from her, and her eyes are fully on me. She picks up on my nuances and words I casually say. She spots when I talk about cliffs and knows when my flashbacks and nightmares are bad. She challenges my negative thoughts and tells me to make regular appointments and that I'm not being any trouble. If you are reading, thank you! And there is no reason that you can't find such an understanding doctor. You may have to explain to the receptionist that you need to see a specific doctor or request politely to have an appointment with another. It's your right and choice. You can even take a friend or relative along for support. He or she will be handy to remind you what advice or support you've been given. Remember that frazzled memory I spoke of?

Don't be afraid to write things down or ask the doctor for a handout or advice sheet. And when you have been given a prescription, take it straight to the chemist and take the drugs at the right time and dose. There is nothing wrong with taking anti-depressants after your catastrophic loss. I'm still taking them seven years later and they help me function during the day and get a good night's sleep, because of their marvellous side-effect of drowsiness.

I also take medicines for anxiety, which has the added effect of reducing my flashbacks considerably, so take those for your PTSD if prescribed. More about those later.

Throughout this book I shall end each chapter with a one or two sentence offering something I'd like you to do or have a think about. I'll end this chapter by encouraging you to ask your GP, or the receptionist, what support groups, counselling, or specialised NHS help are available, either a psychologist or psychotherapist.

CHAPTER 4:

THE POLICE

After months of complaining about nocturnal noises, the police informed us they were caused by someone with a medical condition, and that we wouldn't have to put up with the noises for long. We patiently sat it out and were dismayed when, sadly, the person with the medical complaint died, many months later, and the noises got worse. The police and council seemed powerless to help us. Unfortunately, my mental health deteriorated due to lack of sleep. I snapped and put some enormous signs in my windows that I should not have. I was charged with a breach of the peace because the neighbourhood were stopping in their cars and taking photos for social media. It wasn't my proudest moment, and I'm still ashamed of my actions to this day.

Fortunately, the courts helped again and put me on the path to recovery as part of a diversion scheme aimed at rehabilitating offenders without giving them a police record or jail term.

I also learnt that I could film on my phone the creator of the noise harassment. Until then, I thought it was illegal to film someone, but the arresting police officer told me that the law had recently changed, and I should gather evidence. I charged my phone and iPad up as soon as I got home!

Being interviewed, photographed, and fingerprinted at the local police station was a humbling experience. The kindly desk sergeant gave me a leaflet with places I could go for further help. Noise harassment to people with PTSD is a common issue and I've heard similar stories from other veterans since, and I hope you don't encounter the evil malevolence my family endured. But another very positive outcome is that the courts dropped the charges, provided I accept a referral to SSAFA, the Soldiers, Sailors, Airmen and Families Association. I duly agreed. They explained that this military charity would help me with funding to soundproof my home against the neighbourhood noises, from sources like the Royal British Legion and the Poppy Appeal.

A few days later, I got the evidence the police required, a video clip of my neighbour hammering his wheelie bin lid right outside our kitchen/study and directly under our bedroom. I know, right! What sane person does that! This formed part of my neighbour's ghastly reveille at five in the morning, alongside what sounded like rattling railings and door slamming. The outside noises ceased soon after. We couldn't afford our own CCTV, but an iPad, in our kitchen window, always charged, and with a large memory, proved an adequate deterrent against future outside noises.

The two officers who came to take the evidence were by coincidence the two officers who broke the news of Angus's death to us. On that awful night, they were compassionate and patient and I've nothing but praise for them. It was such dreadful news to convey to us and we were just shocked. We'd come back from a holiday in York but had seen Angus before we departed. He seemed his usual happy self. But he'd been hiding his true pain from us. He'd everything to live for. He had worked his way up to being a night manager at the nearby McDonald's, was on a good salary and was training with them further. He'd a large group of friends and had his own flat in a pleasant area. He was loved by Abigail, Karla, and me.

The difficult thing I wrestle with is that the police didn't tell us there were suicide letters to his friends. Even when I asked them, they said no. Then Angus's flat was locked by the police. A huge bar was bolted to his door and frame and a large padlock was placed there. It wasn't removed until their investigation was completed ten days later. That's when we found the earth-shattering first draft of a suicide letter. Thank goodness for alleged police incompetence, otherwise we'd never have known why he took his life and all three of us would have been blaming ourselves until we go to our graves.

We could view his body at the mortuary, but only for identification and from behind a glass partition. His body was part of the investigation. This was another troublesome part of his death by suicide. We so wanted to hold him. I've washed, dressed, and shrouded many corpses as part of the last offices rites of respect as a nurse. Yet, I couldn't do this for my boy. His post-mortem was delayed by a week, due to there being several murders in Aberdeen. When he was finally released into the care of an undertaker, we were advised not to view his body and to have a closed coffin funeral. Not being able to see or hold him really messed with our heads and delayed the grieving process. Karla doubted he was even in there and spent many sessions with the Cruse Bereavement Care grief counsellor talking about this. I felt like I'd let my boy down again and my self-esteem plummeted.

The officers told me I should ask questions, and I did. The Procurator Fiscal, the court system here in Scotland, much like a coroner, got in touch as part of his investigation and he gently answered our questions. But the big question, for now, was unanswered. Why did Angus take his life?

Getting back to the noise harassment - not all the police were so understanding and many who arrived at our door to hear the noises themselves were abrupt and appeared not to believe us. That all changed once I had the evidence. It was an added stress my family didn't need, being noise harassed during our grief.

I learnt, reluctantly, to accept that the procedures of the police are there to investigate that Angus's death was suicide and not by the hand of another.

If you've got into trouble with the police because of your PTSD, accept your wrongdoings, but keep seeking help.

If you find yourself in a situation where help isn't forthcoming, take a deep breath and gather the evidence. But keep phoning the police or council. That is their duty and if you are being harassed, it's a crime.

If your involvement with the police is because of a relative's suicide or sudden death, then ask questions. You should have been assigned a Family Liaison Officer. Note their direct phone number and call them. They will not mind.

CHAPTER 5:

SSAFA

The Soldiers, Sailors, Airmen and Families Association is a wonderful organisation that helps any veteran, from one day's service onwards and of any rank. This is extended to their children and partners. I've heard of them helping cover the removal costs, finding homes for veterans, and even helping to buy wheelchairs and stair lifts.

The social worker that I was assigned as part of the court's diversion scheme assured me that SSAFA would help me soundproof our home now that our savings had run out. Up to that point, I'd employed a carpenter to install thicker doors and build soundproofing against our lounge, kitchen, bedrooms, and loft walls. We even went as far as getting him to put a soundproof layer in the basement. This all helped dampen down the bangs that sounded like they were coming from the adjoining wall. But we still needed to lower ceilings and install soundproof doors downstairs. I took to the internet and soon found examples of where SSAFA had successfully fully soundproofed houses for veterans with PTSD, so I saw some light at the end of the tunnel as Karla and I tried various earplugs. Abigail slept with her headphones on, playing music, until she moved once the solicitor had handled Angus's estate and she inherited his flat and savings. I thought it was brave of her to sleep in the room where Angus had taken his life. I find it too painful to go there, but she draws comfort from being in his room and has made the place her own lovely home and has had the kitchen refitted and redecorated. She keeps his clothes in one of the built-in cupboards and I wear one of his fleeces, the only thing that fits my larger girth!

I was discharged from the social worker once a SSAFA case worker was assigned and, a week later; I was assessed. I gave my military details such as regimental number, places served, rank and dates of service to a lovely gentleman, who confided to me he too had lost an adult child. He worked in the university where my daughter was studying fine art. He gave me hope that one day, I could lead a working life and feel valuable. To give you hope, dear reader, despite her grief, Abigail passed her degree one year later. This is largely because of her tight circle of friends she made at Gray's School of Art. If you are reading ladies – thank you for looking after Cupcake!

Our finances were tightly scrutinised. The charity has a duty to its donators to make sure every penny is accounted for. But sadly, SSAFA were not to be the funders, instead the case worker worked hard to secure funding from other charities. She worked for months, contacting various army and nursing charities on my behalf. We were dismayed when no help was forthcoming from my Regimental Association. She drew a blank from the Army Benevolent Fund, Poppy Scotland, the Royal British Legion, etc. I wasn't deemed worthy of even one penny.

Fellow veterans were dismayed, too. They told me that their Regimental Associations part funded the soundproofing costs along with contributions from other sources. I guess nurses are not so good at caring for their own. We were at our lowest at this stage. We had little money coming in and were forced to use the local food bank for a few months, and we started selling things from our home on eBay. Ironically, the money from selling my old uniforms fed us when we needed fresh fruit and vegetables.

My self-worth took a major hit. I felt that my military and nursing career hadn't mattered. I hadn't asked for PTSD to engulf me. I didn't imagine these flashbacks, nor make up the nightmares. My mental health deteriorated even more.

I questioned where the money that people put into poppy tins, or donate to the RBL, went. Surely, they would want me to receive help, to make me calm in my home, to help me sleep, to stop the ghastly nightmares and flashbacks. This is when I walked to the cliffs.

CHAPTER 6:
SIGNS OF SUICIDE

I missed the typical signs of suicide in Angus. He didn't appear morose. He hadn't said unusual goodbyes or thanked us for his life.

We hadn't been to his flat for a while because he worked night shifts and came to the family home for a weekly meal. We didn't see how sparse his flat had become. It was only after his death that we realised he'd sold, or given away all his possessions, save for his laptop, phone, game console, and a sparse amount of clothes. All his DVDs, books, computer games, etc were gone. He'd closed all but one of his banks and savings accounts.

There is a box in our loft that we found a few weeks after his death when looking for things to sell on eBay. It was marked 'For Dad.' I cried for hours when I opened it and saw his Star Wars collection, Lego, and Big Finish CDs. I shared these hobbies with him, and he knew how much they would mean to me. I haven't been able to open the box since. But I now feel strong enough to do so and shall enjoy reminiscing as I unpack it. They will be treasured items to pass onto Abigail's future children so that they have something of their uncle's. Angus had sold or given away all his other possessions. This is common amongst those who take their own lives.

Angus had no mental health conditions. He rarely drunk alcohol, nor did he take illegal drugs. None of these risk factors to suicide applied to him.

We found out, weeks after his death, that Angus had quit his job a month before he took his life. He hadn't told us. He was winding down his affairs. It was a firm intention to end his life. Prior to his resignation, he tried to speak to several work friends about his suicidal thoughts. Being young themselves, they didn't know what to say and a few have contacted me to say how sorry they were not to get him the help he needed or to contact us. It doesn't bring Angus back and none of them should feel guilty. They hadn't been trained to handle a suicidal person. Their branch of McDonald's has put them through suitable training since.

The letter we found in his flat once the police removed the locks was handed to them as it spoke of a heinous crime that happened to him a year earlier. It pains me that the culprit is still free to wreak havoc on others and ruin more families' lives. As a family, we blame this person for Angus's death, and he has effectively murdered him. We must reassure ourselves that the police investigated this aspect as best as they could and that we should trust them to have done so.

Not all suicides leave a note. I didn't on the day I decided to end it. It was a snap decision. I just couldn't see an end to the noises and the effect they were having on me. If you are wondering what my crime was to have such harassment – it was for keeping fantail doves in my garden. A peaceful hobby, I thought! And it is, they are beautiful, calming birds, when I get peace to be with them and watch their gentle fluttering and spectacular flights. We released them over Angus's grave during the funeral.

There will be unanswered questions after a suicide. 'Why?' will be the biggest. You may feel that you failed that person, I certainly do, and that will never go away. It comes back to haunt me in my darkest hours. But I shouldn't, and neither should you. My rational side soon takes over and puts me at ease, thanks to the professionalism of a kind psychologist and three counsellors. But look for these signs in others and in your loved ones. It may save a life. Talk, listen, and take them to their GP or out of hours emergency doctor, because this is a crisis, and with the right psychiatric help, they can be saved.

My thought for you? Don't beat yourself up. Know that you loved them and did all that you could.

CHAPTER 7:

THE FUNERAL

The funeral is an important ritual. It's your chance to say a loving goodbye, and it allows others to share in your grief. It's a chance for you to see how loved your relative was.

Shop around for a compassionate undertaker, one who listens to you and can help guide you through the legal requirements, such as attending the Registrar to register the death of your loved one.

Take time to choose the coffin and what you want your loved one to wear. Our funeral director encouraged us to have Angus dressed in his favourite jeans and t-shirt.

We didn't have the chance to view Angus in his coffin, because of the manner of his death. But we asked the staff to place objects with him. When Karla and I were first dating, she made me a cuddly toy duck from the Red Cross shop in the military hospital we were working in. It was my first gift from her, and I cherished it. He was called, imaginatively, Daffy! Wherever I went in my career, Daffy came with me. It garnered some funny looks from the lads in the barracks' rooms, but I didn't care. He was my lucky mascot and kept me safe. He was a reminder of the love Karla and I have for each other. And now Daffy rests with our son, along with the ashes of our dear Bessie, the family dog who the children grew up with when I'd left the army, and we had settled down in Woodbridge, our first non-army married quarter home. Her ashes were encased in a small wooden urn, and I like to think that they are together again, playing fetch or running free, side by side. Both actions brought me comfort.

Visit the undertaker's chapel of rest or resting rooms as often as you need. This is your chance to talk to your loved one and be with them for a last time. If you can, hold their hand, caress their face, kiss them, and stroke their hair. As you would have in life. Kiss them goodbye. Tell them you loved them.

I hadn't realised how expensive funerals were, and this wiped out our savings, that, and the soundproofing work. We did not want the funeral costs coming off Angus's estate; we wanted Abigail to benefit from his money. We felt it was our duty to provide for our son this one last time. I guess I was trying to compensate her for losing her brother. They were so close, and she too has needed professional therapy and guidance. I didn't want her having money problems, too. That was for us, her parents, to shoulder.

If you find yourself in a similar financial situation, then don't be coy about asking the funeral director to defer payment until the estate of the deceased is handled by a solicitor. There are even state grants to help with some costs. The staff can help with this too.

Choose the type of funeral service you want, be that religious or humanist, or something else. We opted for a funeral at the church we attended for years, where the children went to Sunday School and where Karla worshipped. She has since lost her faith in God. We only go to Remembrance Day services now.

We each chose a hymn, and Abigail brought along Angus's favourite song to play.

We didn't specify a dress code for the mourners, but we dressed in black. I wore the black tie that Angus wore for his first job, whilst still at school, as a waiter in the local hotel.

I was touched by the number of his friends who attended and felt guilty that I had not thought to extend invitations to them. Our grief was so consuming that we couldn't shoulder the burden of others. I hope they will forgive me.

I carefully chose his closest friend to carry his coffin out, along with his cousin, uncle, two family friends and Angus's grandfather, despite his continued protests that I shouldn't have barred a specific relative from attending. This was the alleged child abuser that I wrote about at the beginning of this book. I also did not want a relative attending who had screwed me over in business, twice, more fool me. My father and mother have not spoken to me since, nor did they come to pay respects to Karla, Abigail, and me at our family home prior to the funeral. I just received one awful text message. It's no loss. This was about Angus, and he needed those he loved and who loved him there, not some family reunion. Abigail held my hand as we walked out of the church, the coffin on my shoulder.

We opted for a burial, because we wanted a place to visit and pay our respects to Angus. A white dove and an etching of Bessie are on his headstone, watching over him. Karla and I bought the plot, called a lair, next to him. There is room for Karla and me to be buried with Angus and the next plot/lair is for Abigail and perhaps her future family. I pray she doesn't need it for decades. She deserves a long, healthy, happy life after the trauma she has bravely faced.

We booked a function room in our favourite hotel, where we had enjoyed many fine meals with Angus. They looked after our family and funeral guests well with tea, sandwiches, etc. We needed their nurturing.

Take your time in arranging the funeral and have it how you want it, or how your loved one would have.

CHAPTER 8:

COMBAT STRESS

I'd read great things about Combat Stress on their slick website. The reality, for me, was anything but successful. I was referred to them by the caseworker of the court's diversion scheme. It formed part of my rehabilitation so that I would not receive a criminal record. I was grateful and hoped that Combat Stress would help my confused mind. My nightmares were getting worse and living under the oil rig choppers routes caused me no end of flashbacks. I've come to hate the sound of rotor blades, and they still send an ice-cold chill down my spine to this day. It would be over four months before I received an appointment, and this would be in Inverness, over four hours' drive away.

The weather there matched my mood. The sky was heavy-laden with black clouds, which threatened an approaching storm. I was met at the reception of a Poppy Scotland building by a cheerful receptionist who explained that a psychiatric nurse who worked as a locum for Combat Stress had an office here. I was then escorted to a small, rather claustrophobic room, which proved problematic for me. Along the walls were various military helicopters, pilots, loadmasters and even one, directly in my eyesight, of the search and rescue helicopter that was haunting my dreams, along with a sombre-looking loadmaster, much like that fatal day.

My head went into a spin. I was hypervigilant, hyperventilating, and sweating. I felt the overwhelming need to run. I clung to the chair as the room went spinning by, expecting to faint to the floor.

Then the questioning began. I stripped off layer after layer of clothes, as I perspired, under this interrogation. I had to explain, in detail, what I saw in the helicopter, how I had to go in and out, slipping on the floor, from the tides of blood. Having to relive handling the bodies, taking them to the ambulance. Getting shut in the old army ambulance with two corpses, still dripping blood, having nothing to see except their wounds and the parts of aircraft that had gouged and sliced through them. It was an old-fashioned ambulance and did not even have a hatchway to talk to the driver. There was no chair and as the ambulance rocked over speed bumps and potholes, I was thrown across the corpses on the stretchers. I described being shut in, much like I was shut in this office. The journey seemed forever, but in reality; the mortuary was only a few blocks away.

When the other medic finally opened the door, I felt like bolting, but I had my duty to perform and had to lift the corpses off the ambulance and into the morgue. I watched and waited patiently for the investigation team to start their photography. I had to help there and to this day, I can't abide having my photograph taken with a flash. It sets off an unwelcome video in my head. And then, finally, the corpses were shut into the fridges, and everyone departed, except me and the pathology sergeant. We cleaned the floor as best as we could. The blood was everywhere. And then I returned, dazed, back to the classroom. We were being taught, ironically enough, advanced life support by the anaesthetist prior to the fatal air crash. I was sent home.

I looked down and took in the bloodied sight of my boots and uniform. I could feel sea water and blood squelching in my thin, tropical suede boots. They had to be destroyed. My shaking hands were caked in blood. I stripped in the changing rooms, showered, dressed in my shorts, t-shirt and helmet, and cycled home. My soiled uniform in my saddlebag. They were army issue and would have to be exchanged at the clothing store. Proof of damage would be needed. No amount of scrubbing later or cycles of the washing machine could remove the bloodstains. I'd bought the boots, so they were easily replaced the next day at the shoe shop on camp.

The Combat Stress assessor had opened this can of worms and I wanted to flee, to have the tin lid firmly closed again. She handed me a relaxation CD, told me I needed to attend the centre in Ayr, a good six hours from home, for several weeks of treatment. I explained I was the carer for my disabled wife and could not. She promised that I'd get help locally, and then sent me on my way.

I cannot recall the walk to find Karla in a café near to the Victorian Market. Its stunning glass architecture was lost to me. The clouds had broken, disgorging their heavy load, and I got soaked in the rain. I just recall my racing mind, the flashbacks I was getting since seeing the helicopter photos and having to describe what I went through. The urge to cry was overwhelming. I think I did.

I thought that Combat Stress was for the infantry, for those who'd fought bravely for their country, for the gallant Navy who sailed in dangerous waters and for the heroic pilots who fought in the air. I still didn't consider that I had PTSD. How wrong I was! The nurse had effectively pulled the pin from a grenade and thrown it in my head. My brain turned to mush, became fragmented, and there are a few months I cannot recall very well. A time that worried Karla. I went cliff walking. Fortunately, my GP recognised how ill I was mentally and referred me to an NHS psychologist in the local psychiatric hospital. I got no further help from Combat Stress. Nor comfort from the CD.

A few weeks later, I received a copy of a letter sent by the nurse to my GP explaining that a plane crash hadn't happened that year in Cyprus. My mushy, hypervigilant brain had given her the wrong year. Many of my comrades know I was there, but Combat Stress seemed not to believe me. Two months later, I received a phone call from the nurse. There would be no local help for me, and I was discharged over the telephone. I've since heard that this occurred to several veterans. Some even got an unexpected knock on the door and had a doorstep discharge. I felt that my career meant nothing. Karla took to the internct and sent the nurse links to various reports of the fatal crash, including the inquest and local Greek newspapers. She heard nothing back. My mental health deteriorated further.

That said, if you suffer from PTSD, have your GP refer you to Combat Stress, or refer yourself. I have since heard from several veterans who could attend their local branches of Combat Stress, were diagnosed, and treated with EMDR and medication and taught mindfulness and relaxing hobbies, such as photography. I've simply narrated my experience.

CHAPTER 9:

SOUNDPROOFING

The other condition of the diversion scheme was that I would agree to receive help with further soundproofing my home against the loud noises. As I've previously written, I was initially referred to SSAFA, and they worked diligently to seek funding. Each week, the SSAFA case worker would e-mail me with knock back after knock back from charities I thought were there to help veterans like myself. My self-worth took a further nosedive and my mental health deteriorated even more. I was on my bootstraps, with no one to help pull me up. In desperation, I used the overdrafts on several bank accounts to pay for thousands of pounds of soundproofing. Each time the joiner left, after a week's worth of work, the noises lessened. But the high interest rates were crippling, and I couldn't work effectively with my fractured mind. But we were winning the noise harassment war. We'd lost some battles and skirmishes, but now were jubilant. The sedatives from our GP helped too! As did finally finding earplugs that were comfortable enough to sleep in and would block noises.

We sealed every hole we found. I should say at this point that we'd lived in this home, in the same neighbourhood, for twelve years and had never heard noises like this overnight. It was pure harassment. The carpenter put a foot layer of soundproofing material against every wall adjoining the other property. Then he shaped the skirting boards to make it conform with the rest of the room, and sealed the plaster, ready for us to paint. We've lost parts of every room and even the loft and basement. Our fuel bills are lower, as the house is now well insulated and soundproofed. We struggled for four years to pay household bills. We robbed Peter to pay Paul. We transferred money between accounts so that we could afford electricity, but we had no money for food. We swallowed our pride and attended the local food bank for several months. They accepted our food vouchers, authorised by our GP and local Citizen's Support office, and gave us a warming cup of tea and a biscuit. They chatted with us and filled bag after bag with food. Years later, I am one of their staunchest supporters and give them profits from my novels by donating bags of food and toiletries.

If you need to soundproof your home, then my advice is to find a reputable joiner. Word of mouth or from the approved list of your local council is best. Look at examples of their work online, from their Facebook page or website. Check for customer reviews and comments. Then get quotes from several. You should involve SSAFA, The Poppy Appeal, your Regimental Association, or the Royal British Legion – you may have better luck than me. Then weigh up if it is cheaper to move or stay put and soundproof.

We love our house. It's been adapted over the years to meet Karla's disability. I've my man cave, my study where I sit with Lyn by my side and work productively. Karla has her own craft room. She paints the most realistic dog, cat, and horse portraits. It's as if you could stretch out your hand and stroke the animal. They bring a lot of pleasure to their owners. Gwyneth, the Bravehound mascot, owned by the founder, Fiona, is on the back cover of this book. This is one of Karla's paintings.

It would have been expensive to get a new ramp to the house entrance, walk-in bath, and shower, raised toilet, etc. We love this village, it's normally peaceful! The harbour and lighthouse are so picturesque and there are several places to walk a dog and enjoy the scenery.

Besides, the army taught me to not only nurse, but to adapt and overcome. To stand up to injustice and to take the battle to the enemy. There was no way I was going to allow my family to be harassed out of our home.

The noises have gone. They were not all coming from outside. They were originating from the one source where we told the police and council. They did nothing to help my family. Nor did the military charities. Those we were referred to by the court system. I'll no longer donate to the Poppy Appeal – where does their money go? Is it to pay the high salaries of their top echelons? I still wear my poppy badge with pride and remember the fallen. Where does the Combat Stress and the Royal British Legion money go and what happens to people like me, who may not have the support of a loving wife, or don't get the care from another charity like Bravehound? Why did my Regimental Association and the Army Benevolent Fund not come to my aid in my time of need?

Fight your corner, take a step back, assess your living conditions and either move or soundproof. You'll soon get peace of mind and the chance to sleep between nightmares.

CHAPTER 10:

EARPLUGS

You would not believe the number of earplugs I've tried over the years before finding one that causes no pain when I sleep. I like to sleep on my sides. It relieves a lot of my knee pain and I use a small pillow between my legs for support.

I first tried the usual yellow earplugs, like those we got issued in the 1980s, for firing weapons. They were too rigid. So next I tried foam ones, they made my ear canal sore. Then I saw an advert for Specsavers. They could create custom fitted earplugs. They usually make these for the oil rig workers here in the North-East. I was their first customer to get them because of neighbourhood noises. They fitted my ear a treat. But they were designed for someone working on their feet, not lying on their sides. The silicone hurt a lot. They were expensive, too, at over one hundred pounds.

I then tried a hearing centre in Aberdeen. The receptionist told me they could guarantee a good night's sleep, or my money back. They filled my ear with a different material, took mouldings, and presented me with softer fittings. I hadn't the heart to go back and seek a refund – the noises were caused by an exceptional source, and it wasn't the fault of the technician. The earplugs are brilliant for when I'm on my feet, but not to sleep pain-free.

It was back to the internet and a trawl through eBay for different earplugs. Months went by, and my bedside cabinet grew in depth with various earplugs that weren't suitable.

But one day I struck gold. I was shopping in Boots with Karla, waiting for her to choose something and I idly looked across and saw shelves of swimming aids. There, nestled amongst nose plugs and goggles, were earplugs designed to stop water from getting in your canal. They were made of the softest material, like rolling a marshmallow in your fingers. I cheated! They weren't supposed to go right in your ear canal, but were supposed to form a seal around your ear opening, to stop water getting in. Instead of just rolling it into a ball, I pinched the end so that it formed a one-centimetre length, which I gently inserted into my ear canal before sealing. Eureka! It formed a tight seal, and I couldn't hear a thing. Between this chance find, the soundproofing, and the prescribed medications, we had found a solution that helps us hear no noise harassment.

If you find yourself in a similar situation, or your important sleep is interrupted by other noises, such as traffic or fellow houseguests, then try various earplugs until you find the ones that suit you. Sleep is important to help you cope with your grief and to live with PTSD.

CHAPTER 11:

MEDICINES

I've worked my way through the local health shop herbal sleeping products. I've since learnt from my GP that many are not licensed as medicines and could damage my liver. I threw them out. If you have insomnia and your head is ruminating over your loss or actions from your military career, or other causes of PTSD, then learn from my errors and seek an empathetic GP. It took me seeing three locums before I found the GP who understood my needs.

I now take the maximum dose of Pregabalin, 300mg twice a day, for my PTSD. It lessens flashbacks and nightmares. Initially, it made me quite floaty and spaced out, but I soon got used to this. Being a muscle relaxant, it had the added benefit of stopping neck and shoulder pain I have, probably from years of internet and computer work. Though I also think that some of it is caused by the muscle tension of the area from the stress of PTSD.

I am also prescribed the anti-depressant Mirtazapine, again at the high dose of 45mg each night. It knocks me out! It has stopped me from going for cliff walks on my own. Now, I go there to walk Lynne, and she terrifies me by looking over the edge to see if she can chase the birds on the rocks below!

With both drugs, I was advised to slowly build the dosages to avoid side-effects. I can function well through the day and have been able to return to working efficiently, and soon we paid off our overdrafts. Life seems more colourful now. I don't have a grey cloud hanging over me.

I now find that I need to be in bed for nine hours instead of seven. I still get nightmares and have to be woken by Karla or Lynne. We agreed she does this at the start of any nightmare because I once thrashed out and inadvertently hurt Karla. Lynne now sleeps in our room, and she has a clever way of waking me from nightmares. She either nudges me with her nose, or creeps in close, and then sticks her tongue in my mouth! Gawds! I should add that this technique is not endorsed or trained by Bravehound. Lynne thought of this technique all by herself! She's a great comfort to me though and soon chases away my demons. Stroking her soft fur is soothing and helps slow down my heart rate, and she loves the attention. I often fall asleep with her in my arms.

I don't always remember the nightmares, but when I do, they involve the people I cared for in death. But I cope with them thanks to the medicines, and I can get some sort of good rest each night.

My anxiety comes and goes like an unwelcome cloak. It wraps itself around me and crushes my chest to the point where I have difficulty breathing or experience chest pain. Lynne cuddles me tight on the nights when it is high. She cleverly senses this. Other times she sleeps across my feet. The contact is warming and reassuring as I face my demons once more. Neither of the prescribed medicines help control my anxiety. But the day Lynne came to her forever home, it plummeted. Her cuddles are amazing. She radiates peace and stroking her is so soothing. She's the best medicine. We can be seen cuddling throughout the day. Karla, meanwhile, tuts and rolls her eyes! Karla calls her my Mistress!

Don't be tempted to take illegal substances. I've heard that some veterans take cannabis. They swear blind that it helps them sleep and to confront their flashbacks. But it has awful side-effects like reduced brain functioning and paranoia. Besides the trouble with the law. Stay away from dealers or homegrown substances. Instead, find a trusting and sympathetic GP and take their advice and prescribed medicines.

I used to ruminate about Angus in the wee small hours. I'd tie myself in knots about how I should have known he was going to kill himself. I felt I'd failed him as a dad and didn't deserve his love. I'd go over ways I should have helped him. I just wish that he'd have told us, and we could have got him the counselling help he needed.

Do yourself a big favour. Don't play over the 'What ifs?' night after night. Book another GP appointment and ask for help to sleep or a prescription of anti-depressants. Then read on for more ways to help yourself.

CHAPTER 12:

NOISE-CANCELLING HEADPHONES

SSAFA came up trumps with a life-changing offer from Help for Heroes. They could not justify to their finance committee and trustees spending thousands on soundproofing but offered me a top of the range pair of Sony noise-cancelling headphones instead. They proved a lifeline and have changed the way I live, for the better, and Help for Heroes are one of several military charities that I will always support in gratitude.

I'd tried several pairs of headphones to blot out slamming garage doors and bin lids, violently rammed home gates and the noises that seemed to come from the adjoining internal wall. They were around the £60 mark, all that we could struggle to afford. I guess you get what you pay for. None of them stopped me from hearing loud noises.

I was sent, via the local John Lewis shop, a pair of Sony WH-1000M2 headphones and they were, and still are, fantastic. I'm saving up for the M4 model as after four years, these are wearing thin around the headphone material. That's great service though! I wear them all day, from the moment I'm out of bed and they are the last thing I take off before I race Lynne to the pillow. They have a clever button on the side where, once pressed, they immediately switch from noise-cancelling to ambient sound. That way I can hear the sweet murmurings of Karla. And when I don't want to hear her telling me off – I switch back to noise-cancelling! They are a marriage saver too!

These headphones go two stages further. I can programme them, via an app on my mobile phone, to concentrate on voices, and they will still blot out the loud noises. This means that I can also hear the telly and once more relax in my lounge. The other clever thing is that the ambient noise can be adjusted down. I quickly learnt to reduce this to twelve, to block out the bangs.

Overnight, and that's how quick delivery was, Help for Heroes and SSAFA brought me further peace of mind. Thank you!

We live on a bus route and the nearby fish factory has many lorries with loud noises passing by. They are even heard in our house, but the headphones block these out. More importantly, they block out the sound of the helicopters flying the oil workers to the North Sea rigs. My flashbacks reduced significantly.

Karla can now work in her craft room above the lounge, in one of the spare bedrooms, without worrying about me complaining that she's making too much noise, or if she inadvertently drops something. While noise cancelling, I can be in the lounge doing crosswords or listening to the radio. I can even read in the lounge once more, provided I have switched on that reassuring noise cancelling button. I'm looking over my shoulder as I type this. Now don't be telling Karla, but the voice in my headphones that alerts me to what function I've switched on is rather comforting and when her soft tones tell me I'm now entering noise cancelling mode, it's as if an angel is whispering in my ear, to tell me I'm safe. I love her voice.

I'm a huge Radio 4 and 4 Extra fan. I love their comedies and dramas, as well as their fascinating documentaries. I download and listen to various podcasts. I simply tap one side of the headphones and I'm instantly listening to the Navy Lark, Just a Minute or Broadcasting House. These headphones have proved a blessing. The headphones have a special adaptive function which is programmed through their app to the shape of my ears and head to provide the best quality of sound and, more importantly, noise-cancelling. I don't play music often, but when I do, it's like the band is in the room with me.

I love Doctor Who and am a great fan of Big Finish. They produce some brilliant shows from many of the Doctors, including my favourite, Tom Baker. I can buy and download their dramas onto my phone and sit in bliss as I allow the stories to unfold. My imagination journeys into another world and it's very therapeutic, a real mindfulness moment. Other favourites include Dark Shadows and Blake's 7. Try them!

A one-hour charge, while I'm in the bath, lasts me all evening and into the next day, so there is never a worry about the battery running low.

They have lots of padding, so are comfortable to wear.

The major downside is that they aren't suitable to wear when it is raining, otherwise I risk damaging them. Sadly, when I'm out with my fantail doves, someone likes to slam bin lids, rattle railings, ram home gates and shed or garage doors. But I've got round this by inserting my earplugs, then wearing over the ear headphones on a cable direct to my phone with a special adapter. I no longer hear these noises, nor the overhead rotors, above the sounds of the TARDIS and Daleks! The army taught me to take a step back, evaluate and find a new solution, great training that has kept me sane when demented folk are around.

The only other problem I have with this is I can be noise-cancelling while whispering sweet nothings to Lynne whilst we cuddle and Mrs B creeps up behind me and has a face like thunder because I'm not showering her with love! Lynne and I have now learnt to go into the privacy of my study to do this!

I now love being at home, immersed in vintage TV (guaranteed no helicopters) or watching the latest carefully chosen films on Amazon

Prime. A lovely Royal Marine I met on holiday introduced me to Vikings. It's awfully blood-thirsty and is compelling viewing. After a few episodes of their axe-wielding, I switch to some Scooby Doo to rebalance!

If you have PTSD and loud noises start a chain of events in your head, buy the best noise-cancelling headphones you can afford, or reach out to SSAFA and Help for Heroes. The supporters of these charities would want you to get the help you deserve. www.helpforheroes.org.uk

CHAPTER 13:

SLEEP

You've probably gathered from the previous chapters that Karla, Abigail, and I have struggled to sleep because of external influences that we had no control over. Neither did the police and council. It took a few years, but we found solutions and it is no longer a problem.

During the time it was an issue, our mental health declined. Sleep is so important to maintaining a balanced, healthy life. Lack of it can affect your work, your social life, judgements, and relationships. Here are a few tips to help you get as good a night's rest as you can.

Sleep in the coldest bedroom, preferably at around 18 degrees Celsius. Turn down the bedroom radiator, open the window air vents, provided outside noise isn't a distracting factor. Consider reducing the tog rating on your duvet. We have a series of duvets ranging from one through to fourteen which we use throughout the changing seasons.

Read the earplugs chapter.

Do not use your bedroom as an office. Forget all about work whilst you are there. The bedroom should purely be for sleep or sex. Don't worry, I won't be expanding on that subject!

Take out televisions and do not watch telly on mobile devices. You should come to bed in a relaxed state of mind, not thinking about the next scene or what you can watch next.

Think about the décor. Have relaxing pastel colours or subtle wallpaper. We have lavender.

Use subdued lighting. Consider buying the special lamps that have low lighting conducive to sleep. These also have clever lighting that resembles dawn to wake you up gradually. These are better than a sudden, shrill alarm. Especially if you have PTSD.

Buy the best bed you can afford as you may spend one third of your life in it. Go big if you can, give yourself plenty of room. We have a King Size; it gives Lynne room to stretch out! She's a big dog. I know this because whenever we pass children in shops or cafes, I hear them say to their parents, 'That's a big dog!' She's a gentle giant, though.

Choose your pillows carefully. Most now describe what type of sleeper they would suit on the packaging. Look for those that match you if you sleep mostly on your back, side, front, or, like Lynne, are sprawled across the length and width of the bed whilst the humans perch precariously on either edge! There are also those that offer optimal lumbar and neck support.

If your PTSD nightmares cause you to thrash out, consider twin beds. Or sleep without wrapping your arms around each other. It's not worth the guilt of having inadvertently struck a loved one, I know.

Listen to calming and relaxation apps. Their music and sound-effects are specially designed to induce sleep. I'll be writing more about one I use in a later chapter.

If you ruminate in the middle of the night, don't stay there for more than ten minutes. Get up, go to the toilet, make a green tea, then try to go back to sleep.

Turn off your mobile phone an hour or two before bedtime. The same for iPads and other devices. The screens can interfere with your sleep pattern by stopping your body from producing the sleep hormone melatonin. Though you can buy special filters or alter your

40

light settings to prevent this if you really must use your devices prior to bedtime.

Do something relaxing before bedtime. I've always loved doing tapestries. The gentle rhythmic pulling through of the skeins always soothes my mind. I was well-known for doing them in the barrack rooms. I was used to the odd looks of my fellow soldiers and medics. Various dogs, winter scenes and tigers now adorn the walls of our home. My favourite, a wood cabin surrounded by snow, adorns our bedroom wall, and gives me a cosy feeling when I study it.

Have a set routine that your body gets used to. You might even like to have certain rituals. Mine is to give Lynne a bedtime biscuit, so she is distracted before the race to the pillow. Then we lie, heads on one pillow, whilst I stroke her goodnight and whisper how beautiful and clever she is. Meanwhile, over on the other pillow, Karla rolls her eyes, turns over and snores louder than Lynne!

Wear comfortable, loose-fitting nightwear. If your feet get cold, wear socks a size larger than normal. You can buy special gloves that are thin enough to wear in bed but will keep your fingers warm. Some even help to keep your hands soft by working overnight with your favourite moisturiser.

Do not neglect any physical problems that you have that may cause you to wake in the night, such as painful joints. Seek the advice of your doctor for the best pain management. There are now specialised pain clinics to which you can be referred. A team, which can include a neurologist or other specialised consultant, and physiotherapist, will holistically assess you and make a care package based on your needs. There are also specialised sleep clinics if a medical problem, like sleep apnoea, is causing disruptions.

Take your medicines. Most PTSD medicines can also act as a sedative. The same for anti-depressants. I've learnt to take mine at around 2100 hours for optimum sleep.

When you wake from nightmares, try a relaxation technique, like rhythmic breathing or checking in with your five senses. I'll discuss these in a later chapter as I'd like to go in-depth about them. They will be your lifeline.

Get the best night's sleep you can – you'll need it to help win the battle with PTSD and grief.

CHAPTER 14:
COUNSELLING

My astute GP diagnosed my military PTSD on the first consultation we had. She listened better than the other three locums I'd previously seen. I suspected I had it too. I knew it wasn't normal to be seeing people that weren't there. That I knew to be dead. I also knew that it was not normal to feel such a great weight of anxiety. But a huge part of me was still in denial. She also recognised I was not coping well with my grief. I knew that too. Losing Angus to suicide was devastating. It was no wonder my thoughts and actions were racing and all over the place. She referred me to a local counselling service, run by a grief charity that has sadly folded. It is a tremendous loss to the area.

The counsellor I saw was fantastic. She was empathic, a great listener, but also a great challenger. I did not need someone who reflected to me nor someone who would patiently wait week after week until I came to resolve my own issues. I needed someone who would listen for the first few sessions, gain an understanding of me, and then help me. And I feel blessed. That is what I got.

For the first two of our weekly sessions, we talked about Angus and my loss. Then other sessions explored me and my past traumas, as well as continuing our talks about Angus. Then one day, soon after my one session with Combat Stress, it all came pouring out. Our session overran. Fortunately, I was her last client, but she would have been late home that night. Her eyes grew wider and wider as I described the plane crash and compared it to other grisly sights I've seen, or the bodies and body parts I've handled. I've seen and aided in a lot of traumas. An awful lot. I've been the first on scenes when serving overseas and I was part of the emergency teams. I think I over shared! She left the room to talk to her colleague. She came back a minute later and told me I have military PTSD. I argued I had terrible grief. She nodded and told me I had both and needed a specialist counsellor who worked locally with the police, using EMDR, but our talking sessions could still run until the building lease expired in four weeks and the charity closed. She gave me the contact details.

I duly phoned the contact and spoke to a charming lady, but she was fully booked and thought I needed even more specialist care. She mentioned Complex PTSD. Now I knew I was in trouble, if my incident was off the scale, even compared to what the police saw.

I reported this to my GP in one of our regular check-ups. I can look back now and see that this was because she suspected, correctly, that I was a high suicide risk. She kept me alive. She still does. She referred me to the Royal Cornhill Psychiatric Hospital in Aberdeen. I frowned. I just had terrible grief. I was in such denial. She encouraged me to continue with the free counselling sessions.

I found it quite an intimate and revealing process to have someone actively listen to me pour out details about my family life, my emotions, my work life, etc. I would recommend counselling to everyone who has had a loss. She helped me to see that I had PTSD, that I was under a lot of pressure in putting Abigail financially through university, care for her emotionally, care for Karla physically and emotionally, manage the housework, household bills, and then try to cope with my grief and mental health issues.

We talked about Bessie and how much I missed having a dog. She helped me see dogs had always been an active part of my adult life, since qualifying as a nurse, and how supportive they had been to me. She encouraged me to pursue the referral my doctor had made to an organisation called Bravehound. Little did I know I had a challenging year ahead of me. These counselling sessions were a walk in the park compared to the psychotherapy I would have, six months later.

During my sessions with the counsellor, she would look directly at me and say, 'You don't realise just how ill you are.' I brushed these remarks off. I was still in denial.

She would correct me when I said, 'I was just a nurse,' as I brushed aside her attempts to praise my actions. I said this a lot, and she tried to make me see I did good things in my career, before I had to give it up to care for Karla. I didn't believe her. My self-worth was at rock bottom. She kept calling me a hero and I would argue I wasn't because I had no medals and never went to war. She carefully guided me in seeing that I'd attended many training accidents, that I'd seen wounds, burns and amputations that no normal nurse may see.

The same counselling service saw Karla for one session before they closed. This was because I would repeatedly talk about how worried I was that Karla would take her life. Karla has childhood traumas that have developed into serious psychiatric problems since her teenage years. She has twice tried to kill herself since I've known her, and she's described another time before I knew her. The last time she tried to kill herself, she was very near death, and, thanks to the quick action of a care assistant, she was saved. I tried so hard to keep a sense of normalcy at home and to shield the children from it all. It seems a cruel twist of fate that our son would take his own life.

Karla told me she talked about how worried she was about my declining mental health. Now it was her turn to be worried that I would take my life. I hadn't realised. I was in such mental torment about Angus, I couldn't see the effect I was having on poor Karla. I vowed to persevere with the psychology, no matter how painful it got. And it did. But more about that later. It would be later for me too. I had to wait six months before my first assessment. Combat Stress and now my counsellor had opened a large can of worms in my brain, and I did not know how to shut the lid again.

Unfortunately, the counselling service closed a few weeks later because their funding was withdrawn, and they could not afford to lease the building. My counsellor moved onto a children's charity in Aberdeen. I know she will touch many people's lives and help them with their issues. I sent them a cheque as a thank you for the care Karla and I received.

My tip is simple. Losing a child is catastrophic. Any loss is. So is living with PTSD. You will benefit from seeking a counsellor. Ask at your GP surgery if there are any services locally. Some may be free. Our GP practice now employs their own counsellor. In the next chapter, I will discuss the service Karla used.

CHAPTER 15:

CRUSE BEREAVEMENT CARE

Cruse Bereavement Care is a free service, where their specially trained grief counsellors will help guide and support you through your loss. They have centres in most cities throughout the UK. Our local one was Aberdeen, and we tied this in with visiting our favourite vegan café, The Food Story. They make the most delicious coffee and hot pots if you find yourself in the area, and they are dog friendly. But I'm digressing.

You need to wait six months before a self-referral. I guess, as I found out, your emotions are all over the place and, like I did in front of my counsellor, you might spend too long during the session crying. After this wait, you are seen quickly. You may wish to check this is still the case.

Karla was seen by one of their most experienced grief counsellors. I'm not privy, and rightly too, to what she discussed. She attended weekly sessions, and these were extended so that in the end she had over double the number of sessions usually offered. They helped her a lot. Karla confided in me that one aspect of Angus's death that she struggled with was not believing his body was in the coffin that we buried. We were told by the undertaker he wasn't fit to view and so we could not say our goodbyes. It's not the same stroking or kissing a coffin lid. We both needed to spend time with our son's body and because of the police investigation and the time it took for his body to be released to the care of the undertaker, his condition had deteriorated. It was tough for Abigail, too. It hampered all our grieving processes.

Cruse Bereavement Care relies on donations and fundraisers to help with their running costs. The volunteers and counsellors work for free. If you can, please consider leaving a donation.

Unlike other counselling services, you don't need a GP referral. You simply pick up the phone. Their website is www.cruse.org.uk and they also have a helpline you can phone at any time to speak with volunteers. Cruse Bereavement Care is for any form of bereavement, be that a child, parent, sibling, grandparent, partner, or friend.

As with all counselling services, they are bound by strict confidentiality, so you can talk freely about what is on your mind. No one will judge you. The more honest you are with whichever service you decide on, the better I think you will learn to live with your grief. I deliberately will not use the terms 'closure' or 'get over it,' for neither is helpful. Nor is 'moving on' – I especially find this term unhelpful and hurtful. With time and expert care, you will take baby steps and learn to live a new type of life. Take one day at a time. You will be hit with the juggernaut of grief at unexpected times. Let it wash through you and use the coping mechanisms in this book and from your counsellor. And have a good cry, let the tears flow freely, it's helpful to release the emotions. The same for those with PTSD. You'll learn, with the correct therapy, to live the best type of life you can. And you will. Keep reading my book.

For now, put down my book and visit www.cruse.org.uk to check if you can access local support, or give them a phone.

CHAPTER 16:

PSYCHOLOGY

I was assessed by the referral from my GP, in need of psychology. My appointment came about six months later. It was my turn to be a patient of the Royal Cornhill Hospital in Aberdeen, as an out-patient. I settled Karla in the familiar canteen and made my way down their glass corridor. It felt odd to be a patient, rather than visiting Karla on the wards.

My psychologist was my saviour. We sat facing each other for week after week until she healed my fractured mind. I was broken, and she patiently and gently pieced me together. She challenged me when I said I should have coped; I was a qualified nurse. I should have been used to awful sights and tasks. She taught me why the Tornado jet crash event was uppermost in my flashbacks and nightmares.

She told me she works with the Special Forces. I knew I was in expert hands. And importantly, that she knew the military mind and had experience with the army. I could be brutally honest with her and describe things in detail. And I did. When I told her what I had to do, she told me it was off the scale. Even above some of the SF situations. Now I knew it was serious. Whether or not I liked it, I had PTSD. I didn't even disagree with her. We agreed to a treatment plan. I'd read up on my condition and the treatment options, so wasn't surprised when she wanted to perform EMDR. I was her patient for over a year.

The NHS will not accept referrals for bereavement. They consider it a part of life and that people need to work through the grieving process. They recommend getting support from organisations like Cruse Bereavement Care instead. My kindly psychologist let me talk about Angus, though, and she taught me about suicide and the crime Angus experienced. She helped settle my mind somewhat, but it took months of work.

I confided in her about my nightmares. They would be the bodies of my patients, but often meld into Angus's face. That's the point where I usually woke myself up by screaming. During EMDR, visions of Angus rose above the other corpses. It was a harrowing time, but I needed to get better. I didn't want to hurt Karla through a thrashing nightmare again. I needed to get better so that I could care for her. I wanted to work more efficiently again. I had to fight the overwhelming urge to shout out and storm out of the room.

I cried often. I was inconsolable sometimes. Life was grey and meaningless. But gradually, she made me see that life was a gift and worth pursuing. Months later, the colour re-entered my sight.

She made me see I was burnt out. I had come to the end of my tether in trying to look after everyone else but myself. She taught me to check in with my body, to observe how tense it was, how I was holding my breath, tensing my muscles, especially those around my neck and shoulders. I learnt breathing exercises and the importance of doing something for myself each day. She encouraged me to write novels again. You probably recognise her from my novel, One Last War. There is a lot of me in that book. It is said that if you want to understand someone, read his or her novels. My first novels and short stories are about an army nurse with PTSD who sees ghosts. I see phantoms from my past. My last novel is the first in a zombie series. I'm not sure what that says about me now! But it is fun killing them. It lets out my dark side!

She taught me there is always the one mission that breaks a soldier after an accumulation of horrific duties. That's why I was seeing other dead people. She was surprised that my PTSD hadn't manifested earlier. It had – I just hid it well until my world went crashing down after losing Angus. Bessie, my beautiful, black, flat-coated retriever, had helped keep me sane, and I was lost without her. I yearned for Bravehound to match me with another four-legged companion.

After the plane crash, I was straight home and spending time with Angus. He was born the month before. Now, there were similarities. I think having to identify Angus at the mortuary was the catalyst. I had spent too much time in army mortuaries and not enough in the one where I wanted to be handling Angus. I needed to feel his cold hand, to make his heart restart, like I'd done for countless strangers. I needed to know that he was dead. Yet I couldn't.

When I got home after the crash, I stripped and had another shower. I put my uniform through countless cycles of the washing machine. No amount of scrubbing seemed to get the blood off me and my work clothes. The psychologist talked about my need to be clean since.

I was shut in the ambulance, unable to get out, away from the blood-dripping corpses. Now I can't abide people behind me. I rarely go to shops, but when I do, I perform 360 degrees, turn in the queue, constantly checking on the other customers. Like most veterans, I like to see all around me in cafes. I sit so that I can see the entrance and always need to know where my exits are. I rarely fly, but when I do, my anxiety is sky-high. During our sessions, I was taught relaxation techniques. I'll share these with you in later chapters.

We had a dog called Bouncer, whilst stationed in Cyprus. We adopted her from the dog kennels in the nearby army camp at Episkopi. It was aptly called BARC – British Animal Re-homing Centre. The agreement was that you'd look after the dog as a family pet during your tour of duty and then either pay the huge shipping costs back to the UK or return them for another family to adopt. I took Bouncer for a long walk that day. The coastal paths down to our favourite bay soothed my racing mind. As did our dip in the Mediterranean Sea. My psychologist quickly assessed my need for a dog and acted as another referee for Bravehound. I badly needed the comfort and companionship of another canine friend. I miss Bouncer and Bess. Two very special dogs.

I had low mood dips during the EMDR sessions that would haunt me for weeks. I found the therapy tough. I was made to remember the event in graphic detail. It was as if I was there again. These were worse than the flashbacks. But I persevered. The thought of having another dog gave me something to hang on. And I clung to this dream tightly. My nightmares got worse. I was made to recall things I'd done and seen that I'd kept shut in a box, with a huge chain and padlock wrapped around it and stored in the deepest recesses of my mind. Under the gentle guidance of my psychologist, we explored them together, and in time, it was as if looking down from above, rather than first in the thick of it and then alongside my younger self. She knew when we should pull back, or when to explore further.

There are still parts of the event that I cannot recollect. I only recall lifting one broken body from the blood-soaked helicopter. Then there is a gap until I helped carry a body to the ambulance. I was taught that my mind would have blocked me from remembering certain aspects because of the ghastly nature of my tasks. It was acting in self-preservation. They came back to haunt me at night instead.

I learnt to manage my grief and PTSD, to live with them as constant, unwanted companions. I was glad when I was discharged. I hadn't the heart to tell the psychologist that I was still having nightmares and flashbacks. They are part of me now and I live with them the best way I can.

Consider requesting a referral to an NHS psychologist or psychotherapist if you have PTSD. If you feel that Cruse

Bereavement Care has not resolved your negative feelings surrounding your loved one's death, then think about paying for a private psychologist or psychotherapist intervention.

CHAPTER 17:

EYE MOVEMENT DESENSITISATION AND REPROCESSING

I read a lot of the literature surrounding Eye Movement Desensitisation and Reprocessing. Expert opinions are split over its effectiveness in the treatment of Post Traumatic Stress Disorder. I would urge you to research EMDR and form your own opinion. My views are that it works. I believe it helps focus your thoughts and the exploring of the events and gaining an understanding, through guidance by the therapists, helps your memories to be carefully rebalanced. My flashbacks were bad. So bad that I wanted to kill myself. Now they are manageable. I still have suicidal thoughts, but my rational mind and Lynne chases them away.

I try to avoid the stimuli, my triggers. I pray I never have to step into another mortuary in my personal life; I avoid flash photography, the back of ambulances (unless Karla has one of her spectacular falls!) and I wear my headphones continuously. They are especially helpful in blocking out the sound of the oil rig helicopters that fly over my home. I'd urge you to compile a list of your triggers, talk them over with a trusted friend or loved one, and see how you can change your life to avoid them. Adaption is a helpful coping mechanism.

My nightmares are not constant throughout the night. Before EMDR, I would get them as I was dropping off to sleep. My crying out would wake me, then the cycle would repeat throughout the night. When I woke, they would still be so vivid in my memory. I would be shattered and hyper-vigilant. After EMDR, the hyper-alertness has lessened, though my medication was increased at the same time. I would be asleep for hours at a time and wake up sort of refreshed. Though sometimes I need an afternoon nap in my armchair. Even then, my nightmares won't allow me time off.

Eye Movement Desensitisation and Reprocessing has its origins in the treatment of Vietnam War veterans. It involves sitting near a psychologist as a pinhead light, or two fingers, is moved horizontally. The patient must follow these as the therapist alters the speed. In my case, I responded better to the therapist sitting in front and to my right whilst waggling her fingers. They can go quite fast, and I'd liken it to perhaps being hypnotised. She gently talked to me and asked me to close my eyes and to recall the events that troubled me.

Rather than get you to be straight back into the thick of it, she asked me to recall standing at the helipad, waiting for the all clear to proceed from the loadmaster. Then, over the course of a few months, we progressed to the grizzlier parts. I've sanitised this book as much as possible, so shall save you descriptions of what I saw and had to do. It wasn't pleasant.

The first time I shut my eyes, after following the therapist's requests, I wanted to leap from the chair and storm out of her office. What I saw in my mind frazzled my brain. I had a rush of emotion, cried, and tried to follow her instructions. She guided me to the safety of our agreed safe space. This was explored in a previous session, and I chose the sanded bay in Akrotiri coast that was known to a select few. I miss that spot. Whenever I went there with Bouncer, we had the place to ourselves, and I could strip off and have a swim in the deep, clear blue Mediterranean Sea with her — always wary of her sharp claws in my sensitive parts! My therapist had to guide me there a lot.

I didn't tell her about the skinny dipping. That was Bouncer's and my secret!

Prepare yourself to be bombarded with smells, not just sights. In my case, it was the familiar burnt coppery smell of fresh blood mixed in with the sharp salty tang of sea water. Far too much of it. I desperately wanted to wash my hands. Even now, when I am hyper-anxious, you'll see me rubbing my hands on my trousers. I've swapped this ritual with running my hands through Lynne's soft fur. She'll never complain at the added attention. Her soft, silky fur soothes my troubled fingers and mind.

If you were the one to have found your loved one after their suicide, then you may have PTSD. Please seek the help I've described above. As should any veteran or serving military personnel.

Accept EMDR therapy from the NHS or Combat Stress and persevere with it, no matter how tough it gets.

CHAPTER 18:

HOLIDAYS

Another thing I'm most grateful to the psychologist for is for suggesting to me I needed a holiday. When I told her I couldn't afford one as I'd spent the family savings on soundproofing, she taught me about the various free holidays available to the bereaved and those who'd served in the military. She advised me to search online for them and to apply straight away.

I found several, and for two years, Karla and I were off somewhere new every few months. It did us both the power of good being away from our daily lives. Grief still came with us, as did my unwelcome friend PTSD, but we had the chance to relax, explore new surroundings, and be a couple again. It brought more colour to our eyes. Losing Angus really made us see life in grey. It's an unusual thing. Perhaps it was our deep depression, or it may have been that we both wanted to die and be with our son. Fortunately, the people we met on our various holidays brought us cheer and a desire to live once more.

The first holiday was via SSAFA and was from the suggestion of Lee, the assessor from Bravehound who had been on this holiday himself. It was Holidays for Heroes Jersey, a charity started up by a charming couple called Dawn and Richard who, upon seeing the effects of the war in Afghanistan, wanted to do something for the military and their families. They knew the idyllic paradise of Jersey would soothe their souls. The first holiday recipients stayed in Dawn and Richard's home, a selfless commendable act. Since then, they have provided holidays in a top hotel for thousands of veterans, their spouses and partners, and their children. Their generosity has touched many souls.

Once again, I struggled with the label of hero. I felt I didn't deserve this holiday, not compared to the acts of bravery my fellow veterans were talking about. I felt I was taking away a place from a real military hero. But soon, I saw that my illness was as bad as theirs. Most had PTSD, as well as physical disabilities and issues. All were cracking on with life and finding enjoyment. I learned my symptoms were as common as theirs, but they had learned to manage theirs and they kindly taught me to recognise my condition and deal with it. I was heartened to hear that they had a better experience with Combat Stress, the Poppy Appeal, the Royal British Legion, and their Regimental Associations. They had been helped with vocational courses, retraining and housing. They made me see that my fellow veterans valued the care they had received from army nurses like myself. My chest soon swelled. I knew, deep down, I'd helped thousands of patients. All nurses are heroes.

Holidays for Heroes had the right balance of organised events and outings, time to spend with your family, and meals throughout the day at a long, reserved table where we could gather, chat, laugh and have fun. It was interesting to see that it was right by two exits and one side was by a reassuring wall. Dawn and Richard had given much thought to our needs.

I still find it painful to be around children. It is a reminder of my loss, but it was nice being amongst families and getting to know them. I wish I'd spent more time with them, but I was still rather unwell at this point and needed some solitary time, so I didn't attend the nightly after dinner entertainment, nor the swimming pool and leisure centre. I couldn't cope with the loud music and other noises. It was a glorious holiday though, and Karla and I made some fantastic memories. It was so lovely to see Karla laugh and smile again. I never thought either of us would enjoy life after losing Angus. I still donate to Holidays for Heroes Jersey whenever I can.

We were treated to pub lunches, as well as our breakfast and evening meal, at the first-rate hotel. We had a coach tour around the island and then volunteers kindly ferried us in their cars around the major tourist points throughout the week's stay. So we went to the zoo, the castle and World War Two museums, tunnels, and visitor experiences. We even went to the local hospital, thanks to Karla trying to fight with a German bunker by head-butting it during a night guided tour! Barney, our kindly driver, took her back to get her eye seen by a specialist after her previous A&E visit by ambulance the night before. The bunker won and is still standing! Karla's blurred vision soon righted itself and I'm thankful she can still see how handsome I am and how lucky she is to be married to me!

I proudly wore my gifted Holidays for Heroes polo shirt and still wear it with pride. I was even gifted a branded beanie hat that is lovely and warm against the biting Aberdeenshire wintry winds. Both are a reminder of just how special Dawn and Richard, the volunteers, and Jersey are.

One especially thoughtful day out was a lads' excursion to a massage centre. All the wives and girlfriends went in the morning for relaxing massages, and then we all swapped over. We were fussed over by some kindly ladies who plied us with tea and homemade cakes while we chatted as we waited for our turn to have a massage. By chance, the lady I spoke with was a fellow former army nurse. She understood why I had PTSD and listened as I described the loss of Angus. I'll never forget her kindness, nor the delicious cakes! I gained a stone in weight on that holiday. The massage was lovely. Many knots in my shoulders and neck were unknotted, and the therapist used some calming lavender oils. Even if the smell may mean a manifestation from a Grey Lady – read my first novel if you don't know what I'm blethering on about!

I often listen to the CD I received in the welcome hero goody bag. It's from Jersey musician Gerald Le Feuvre and it helps calm me as I sit back and relax and remember the kindness of strangers.

Dawn and Richard, their fellow volunteers, and the other veterans made me realise that in my small way, I too was a hero and I started to value my military and nursing career. This resulted in a change in my mindset and washed away the negativity that came from being rejected by Combat Stress, Poppy Scotland, the Royal British Legion, and my Regimental Association.

www.holsforheroesjersey.com/

Brother Anthony is a monk who has set up an apartment on the Island of Bute here in Scotland. It is for the bereaved, for those who have lost a child. It's named after his brother, who sadly died at a tender age. John Paul's Retreat is a haven, and we have been blessed to have gone twice.

There is something special about islands, and something magical about Bute. It's a short ferry ride away in the car. The magnificent Victorian train station is next to the ferry terminal. Like Jersey, it is a small island, but packed with lots of places to visit. Go to Mount Stuart, it's the most striking building you'll ever see, set in picturesque gardens. It was used as a military hospital during the First World War.

Brother Anthony lets out the apartment for free. All you need are your meals. There is a fully fitted kitchen, one bedroom, (though I think he lets out his own apartment in the other block to larger families), and a large lounge and dining area. It's so homely and comforting. Do look out for Angus's photo on the wall if you go there. Karla made the frame, and the surrounding craftwork represents things that were special to him.

Booking is by self-referral. Brother Anthony has even extended an invitation for Abigail to go. He's splendid company, and we joined him for a meal in the local hotel where we talked about grief and shared common feelings. He helped heal Karla and me.

We also visited the local Rock n' Roll restaurant, which is tastefully set like an American diner. It's fun looking around and seeing various memorabilia and photos from the 1950s and 60s. Their milkshakes and burgers are divine.

The Isle of Bute opened their arms and welcomed refugees from war-torn Syria and as a result, many of them set up businesses there. Some became barbers, whilst others set up restaurants and take-aways. The best cake and coffee shop along the promenade is run by such a couple.

The apartment is ever so quiet and great for contemplation. Karla enjoyed sitting doing her scrapbooking crafts and jigsaws whilst I sat reading my Doctor Who magazine. From the visitor book, we saw that bereaved mums and dads equally took solace from the apartment, the healing power of Bute, and the comfort from spending time with Brother Anthony, one of God's earthbound angels.

My favourite part of this holiday was sitting and relaxing on the seafront, amongst the local public gardens, looking out to sea. There is something comforting about water. Do visit the local parks, one has a huge aviary with assorted birds.

The second time we were there, we were shown around the Shinty club and later attended their dinner dance. We were guests of honour as John Paul's Retreat sponsor them. We were able to give a small speech about suicide and then presented the various sports awards to the players. We met some lovely young people that night. We even got to talk on the local radio station about John Paul's retreats and the effects of suicide.

We hope to return one day with Lynne, so we can enjoy the forest and seafront walks and introduce Brother Anthony to my furry bundle of energy.

www.johnpaulretreats.org

Daz's Den was donated by a remarkable couple who lost their son to the war in Afghanistan. They created, with the help of the Me and Dee charity, a chalet in the seaside town of Mablethorpe in Lincolnshire. They wanted to honour their soldier son by helping veterans and their families to have a free and relaxing holiday. There aren't many perks to having PTSD, but this was one I qualified for. It's a super chalet with two bedrooms, a shower, a lounge, and a kitchen. There is a decking area to enjoy the Lincolnshire sunshine, and I sat, catching rays, while reading another Doctor Who magazine. It was great to chill and relax. We kept the double patio doors open as we ate meals. The bed was so comfortable and the area was so quiet. I slept; nightmare free, for the first time since losing Angus. It was remarkable.

Our point of contact was a lovely lady called Maria, and she thoughtfully left a welcome pack that included a lion teddy bear, a guardsman toy made by the Dumpling Doll company, a necklace, an attractive bottle to fill with sand from the beach and a well-crafted wooden box. I treasure these items. The guardsman sits on my desk as I type, watching over me, keeping me safe. The lion sits on the nearby bookshelf, wearing my QARANC beret, and the box contains nick-nacks from my service days. I also received a touching poem I read whenever I am distressed. It helps calm me. I wear my Daz's Den poppy badge each November as I remember the fallen. I often think of Daz and his family and their remarkable gift to many veterans and their families. They helped soothe my troubled mind.

Maria had booked a seaside hut with deckchairs which overlooked the sea and beach, and the back overlooked the small railway ride and parks. Karla and I had many cups of tea in our chalet, walks along the sanded beach, and strokes with the donkeys. Our daily ice-cream cones were such a treat and tasted even better by the seaside. This holiday helped soothe Karla's troubled mind too. She keeps the sand bottle on her desk and wears the beautiful necklace. Maria is often in our thoughts. Her charity, Me and Dee, provides holidays for people living with disabilities and their families and will also be a recipient of the profits from this book. She is often in my thoughts. The world is full of thoughtful and caring people like her who want to help, and we are most grateful to her and Daz's family for the opportunity to get away, be a couple, and enjoy life once more.

Sadly, I've learnt that Maria no longer runs Daz's Den, and I can't find reference to it online to point you to. Maria's website is at

www.meanddee.co.uk

When Karla left the military, she still qualified for medical treatment when we were posted overseas to Cyprus. She only needed it when she fell pregnant, and both our children were delivered by QA midwives and a charming RAF midwife who had such a caring bedside manner and loved all the babies under her care. I feel blessed I could attend both births. This Squadron Leader midwife would call me whenever I was on duty at The Princess Mary's Hospital in RAF Akrotiri on the ward above the maternity unit with progress reports about Angus and Abigail and send up photos of them in the lift with amusing comments! But Karla was unhappy about one aspect of her care – she hated being called a Wife Of! That was her acknowledged rank/status by the military, and she rebelled against it and insisted she was a Mrs - she didn't get her own way.

She was delighted years later when she was put in touch with the Not Forgotten Association by one of her student nurses' colleagues who had risen to the rank of colonel and was the Colonel Commandant of the QARANC Association. Her friend, (now a brigadier, made a Dame, and has had an amazing career in the QARANC), put her forward as a guest of the NFA Buckingham Palace Garden Party to which Princess Anne, their Patron, would be attending. I was invited to tag along as her plus one and Husband Of – Karla relished the shoe being on the other foot for once, getting a taste of how she felt. I didn't mind; it was a great day out. Karla wore a pretty dress and fascinator and looked beautiful, as always.

I found it overwhelming being surrounded by military heroes and had to have a turn around the Queen's gardens to calm my emotions. I hope Her Majesty didn't mind us traipsing around her stunning oasis of calm in London. My emotions got the better of me and I cried, something I seem to do at the drop of a hat these days. I hope I didn't spoil Karla's special day out.

The cakes were amazing. You've probably gathered that sugar is a terrible craving I yielded to as a comfort food after losing Angus. My weight ballooned over several years.

We met celebrity guests there, such as the singer Alfie Boe, who I have admired since seeing him on television at the Royal Albert Hall Remembrance Ceremony. Karla managed a selfie with her Gogglebox favourite, Stephen. It's a photo I cherish as it captured her smile that made me instantly fall in love with her from our student nurse days at the Queen Elizabeth Military Hospital in Woolwich. The Not Forgotten Association made us feel like an important part of the military community again.

I wrote to thank them and explained about losing Angus and how it heartened me to see Karla smile once more. I'd looked around their website after buying some items from their online shop – they sell top quality polo shirts and their emblem is an elephant, a mammal that Karla is daft about. Our house is full of elephant themed items. I'm just as bad. I have a shrine to Doctor Who in every room. While viewing their website, I saw they organise many activities ranging from hiking, canoeing, paddle-boarding and other dinner parties at locations like St. James Place. I spotted that they have a relaxing holiday in Spain, in a villa kindly given to them by a sponsor. I asked if Karla could be invited. They readily agreed and once more I became a Husband Of.

Spain was enchanting, and it truly was a relaxing holiday. We gathered at Heathrow and were met by serving Royal Marine Regimental Sergeant Major Glen, who is the nicest of men. He organised our activities all week and ensured we got there safely. Glen spent the week driving us around the island, even expertly taking Karla and other disabled veterans up a steep, treacherous hill so that they could visit the monastery. I had to swallow painkillers and walk! Glen is a gifted artist and when he wasn't kept busy by us would get out his paintbrush.

Once more, we were in the caring bosom of the veteran community and got to know others living with PTSD and physical issues. Colour bloomed in our eyes once more and we were cared for by Rosie, the Head of Events who is the most charming and dedicated soul who loves her veterans like cherished friends. We met volunteers, Dale, and Johnnie, two remarkable men who ensured that all our needs were met. All were expert cooks, and we met in a vast barn each night and ate, drank, laughed, rejoiced, and made new friends. Their fry up breakfasts are legendary. I even met another former QA, and she was a fan of my novels! She was great fun.

There was a pool, lots of recliners and glorious sunshine. I took advantage and read some more Doctor Who magazines.

If you have a disability, regardless of whether it is from your service days or a medical issue once a civilian, the Not Forgotten Association will welcome you with open arms and put you in contact with fellow veterans and find activities you can take part in. We weren't forgotten by them and a year later received a stunning jigsaw from a painting of a Buckingham Palace Garden Party. Karla loved doing this thoughtful gift. Please check them out if you are a veteran.

www.thenotforgotten.org

Two years later, we were invited to stay in a stunning villa in France, called Maison10 in Nyons, hosted by a lovely couple, Sarah and Tim, who are a trustee of the charity. Once again, we were reunited with the lovely Rosie, Dale and Johnnie who nurtured us, along with some brilliant company of fellow veterans. We had a great time, relaxing around the villa, their pool, walking in a vineyard, attending the local market, and watching the stubborn Karla free-falling from an electric bike! This was during an organised trip around the countryside, only Karla hadn't ridden a bicycle for over thirty years and thought the ideal way to get off a bike would be to suddenly stop and then allow it to go flat on the ground, with her still on it! Fortunately, she gave up after almost flattening an innocent woman walking on the pavement. She went off to a café with Sarah while I continued the ride with the others and got saddle-sore, but it was worth it. I hadn't been on a bike since getting Lynne and missed the fresh air. The French countryside was stunning and the electric bike did all the hard work in the glorious heat and welcome sunshine.

Though I missed my Lynne and had to put her in jail (the local kennels) I wasn't without the company of a dog. I'm looking over my shoulder as I type this, so Lynne doesn't read. Sarah and Tim have a gorgeous golden retriever called Mable who enjoyed the attention I lavished on her. She was a cutie!

Johnnie and Dale once more cooked us some delicious food, especially their bruschetta, which would have given any restauranteur a run for their money. Dale bought me some alcohol-free, no sugar lager, so I could have sociable drinks with the others. They tasted just like normal beer and were so refreshing in the hot French sun.

Rosie invited us to another event a few months later. This was a concert in a field at Ballindalloch Castle. Lynne's nose was working overtime when she got a whiff of the hog roast, which was super tasty. We had many refreshing drinks, cake, and a concert with some talented singers. It started off with some gentle 1960s music and the visual treat of dancers in long swishing skirts, then a tribute act to Cher and Freddie Mercury came on. It was great fun and Karla was delighted to win a box of chocolates in the raffle and some posh biscuits in the singing bingo game.

These concerts are held nationwide, so there could be one near you.

If you can afford a holiday and can take time off work, then consider regular holidays and weekend breaks. It'll refresh you and give you a zest for life again. If you are a veteran reading, then please contact the charities I've described. They want you to be treated to these days out and holidays. You've served your country and deserve it.

Those who are bereaved equally deserve time away, and Brother Anthony will welcome you getting in touch, as will Maria of the Me and Dee charity for those affected by disabilities and their families.

CHAPTER 19:

THE COMPASSIONATE FRIENDS

The Compassionate Friends are a supportive charity for those bereaved who have lost a child, sibling, or grandchild. They have an informative website at www.tcf.org.uk and a set of peer-supported Facebook groups where you can chat online with parents, brothers, sisters, and grandparents who have experienced the loss of a child. Their sets of leaflets and bereaved support packs are incredibly helpful and can give you advice and further avenues of support. They also have a helpline where you can phone and speak to specially trained peers.

The Compassionate Friends also run support groups in local areas and some volunteers are trained befrienders, called grief companions, who can provide one-to-one support. Please do contact them.

They also run weekend retreats across the country, one day gatherings and other events. Each is specific to the type of death such as road traffic accident, suicide or drug and alcohol related. Please don't be put off by the cost if you are on a low income because they sometimes offer scholarship awards that meet these costs. We were offered a place at their Birmingham retreat, and although it was a long drive, we took advantage of it. It was held in a magnificent building that was a former home of Mr Cadbury of the chocolate family, and is now

Quaker owned. There was plenty of parking and we were met with welcoming hugs by the facilitators: all were bereaved mothers and fathers who had been trained to support and guide us. We had our own bedroom, like a top-rated hotel, and all meals were provided, including bedtime hot chocolate and biscuits. The quaker corn bread was divine.

The weekend was a mixture of organised talks, activities like crafts, massages, and how to write poetry. There was even one-to-one counselling with a trained counsellor. The candle lighting ceremony and learning the importance of saying the name of our child to others were beneficial to Karla and me. The talks and discussions helped give us a greater understanding about suicide, the effects on our minds and bodies, and how to live more effectively. One facilitator had lost both her children to suicide and could lead a fruitful life aiding other bereaved parents. All gave Karla and I hope about our future and that of Abigail's.

During one craft session, Karla produced a memory glass candle holder with a photo of Angus surrounded by beads and shells. It sits on our lounge bookshelf.

Peer support is powerful. Only another bereaved mother or father can truly comprehend the heart-achingly painful hollowness caused by suicide or other sudden death. Many made friendships which I'm sure will last for life. Don't be put off if you live by yourself. There were many single mums and dads who arrived on their own but left with many friends' phone numbers and Facebook details.

TCF also runs retreats for bereaved siblings and grandparents. Many parents gave testimony to how helpful their children had found them. Some parents return to retreats each year.

If you are lucky enough to go to the Birmingham one, make time to stroll through the extensive gardens and walk around the lake. I went there each morning with a flask of coffee and watched the sun rise and had mindfulness moments with the ducks. It really is a special place, and I can see why the Quakers took over the place.

If you have lost a child, brother or grandchild suddenly, please put down this book and visit The Compassionate Friends website, browse around, see what help is available locally, or when the next retreat is to be held and book a place. Then send requests to join their Facebook groups to receive peer support.

CHAPTER 20:

SAY THEIR NAME

You will not upset me if you mention Angus's name or talk about him. I enjoy hearing people's memories of him. Some folk act like they are in a bad sitcom, like Basil Fawlty in his hotel, trying not to mention the war to his German guests. They tiptoe around the subject. Conversely, there are survivors of suicide who don't like to mention their relation's name. Please don't be like that. Own it. Say their name with pride. It isn't committed suicide anymore, there has been no crime. There should be no stigma attached to suicide. Though sadly, some family members no longer speak to Abigail, Karla, and me – they are no loss, they are emotionally bereft. Own the name of those who have taken their life and talk freely about him or her.

I first heard the phrase, Say Their Name, at The Compassionate Friends retreat. The speaker encouraged us to say the name of the relative who took his or her own life, not to encourage whispered tones. Over the course of the weekend, those who found it painful to talk about their dead child were expertly guided to say their name and talk, many for the first time, about their pain and loss. All of us were saying the name of our child by the time we left. We were taught that it is healthier to do this and that it will benefit our future mental health.

Karla and I learnt it was common amongst parents who have lost their child to suicide to be shunned by friends and family. Some described how best friends now cross the street, rather than talk to the survivor. Others talked about family members who no longer telephone, come over to their house and even answer the phone or doorbell when called upon. In my case, my father stopped speaking to me on the day that we broke the news to him that Angus took his life. I received one rather awful text and then nothing more. All because I asked that a family member who had allegedly sexually abused another family member, not come to Angus's funeral. It's no loss, nor is not having phone calls or visits from my mother. I desperately needed a paternal or maternal handhold or arm around my shoulder to lessen the burden of grief; but none was available, not even at Angus's funeral. They were the only family members who did not release one of my white doves at the graveside. This lack of care weighed heavily on me and contributed to my deteriorating mental health. I was busy caring for Abigail and Karla, but had no one to care for me.

An outstanding example of what to do when you first see the survivor of suicide came from our friend Jonathon. He was a pal from our army student nurse days and was in Karla's group. We were at a reunion in Birmingham and were feeling trepidation about seeing her friends. It was our first social gathering since Angus's death. Jonathon stood up from the table, walked towards us, gathered Karla up in a great big comforting hug, then did the same to me, and said how sorry he was to learn of Angus's death and asked how we were. He then sat us down, ordered us some drinks and chatted about our health, our mental health, Angus and Abigail, and then the others in the group chatted away to us. He's a remarkable man and now works in mental health and I bet his patients have the best of care.

Regarding my military PTSD, I have etched in my mind several names from the more traumatic deaths. I often think of them, especially on the anniversaries and on Remembrance Day. I had tried to forget their names, to put all those memories in a box. Now, however, I've found it healthier to acknowledge them and honour their memory. I say a brief prayer in my head during the minute's silence. When I see them during flashbacks, I acknowledge their presence and perform the coping mechanisms I'll talk about in later chapters.

I'd like you to pause for a moment, remember your relative or deceased comrade, though I'm sure that, like me, they are never far from your thoughts, and then say their name aloud. From now, I'd like you to talk about him or her freely, whenever you feel the need.

CHAPTER 21:
PHOTOGRAPHS

Some relatives find it painful to have photographs of their lost loved one around their home. I explored this in my novel, Group. It's the same for military folk who have lost a comrade. Photos can be a constant reminder of a painful past, rather than a comforting presence or a catalyst for happy memories. As a condition of the retreat, we were told to bring a photograph of the child who'd taken their life. There were some parents who could not view a picture of their child since their death. There were many tears as we placed the photos on the table.

Since Angus took his life, I have found looking at his photographs painful. I get a sudden rush of emotions and either burst into tears or have very moist eyes. I can't speak for a while. This doesn't stop us having photos of him and Abigail around the house, his family home. It sounds a contradiction, but they bring comfort, to see him happy throughout his childhood and early adult life, until the crime. I often blame myself, and wonder, if I'd been a better dad, whether he would have confided in me. I would have got him the help he needed and deserved. The NHS psychologist who treated me informed me he would not have, perhaps through shame, told us of the crime. He would have felt low self-esteem and would have kept his awful experience secret, especially from us. He was protecting his mum, sister, and me. Perhaps that is why I find it so painful to hear a child cry – I imagine the turmoil and pain he would have been in for the last year of his life. He hid his pain so well from Abigail, Karla, and me.

The importance of being able to look at photographs was acknowledged at the retreat and their craft sessions centred around creating jars or photo frames to house our most cherished of pictures. I commend Brother Anthony of John Paul Retreats for encouraging parents to gift the apartment with a photo for the wall. Our memories are valuable gifts.

Take photos of your fallen comrade to reunions and share them around your group. Keep them readily at hand to view when you feel the need.

Cherish the gift of life of your child, brother, relative, friend or comrade and keep their memory alive by looking at their photographs. Give them pride of place on the wall, mantlepiece or your bedside table. Add them as a screen saver on your laptop, PC, tablet, or mobile phone.

CHAPTER 22:

BRAVEHOUND

There were two game changers for me on my road to recovery after hitting rock bottom. The first was the brilliant NHS psychologist who pieced my mind back together and the second, which revolutionised my lifestyle, was, and still is, Bravehound. I badly needed a dog, and they provided me with a furry companion who walks beside me, sleeps by me, watches over me, and is my faithful friend. Every military veteran needs a buddy, and for me, a four-legged companion transformed me back into a functioning person.

Fiona MacDonald is the founder of Bravehound and takes an active part in the organisation. She has her own best buddy called Gwyneth, a gorgeous Scottish Terrier. She's the emblem and mascot of Bravehound. You can see photos of her at www.bravehound.co.uk

Fiona recognised the healing power of dogs and had a clear vision for this military charity. She and the team match a dog with a military veteran living with PTSD and/or other mental health conditions as either a companion dog or as an assistance dog.

I hate going out. I detest going to shops, restaurants, pubs, etc. My anxiety levels go sky-high. I dislike being around people. I loathe loud noises, especially bangs. My assessors, Lorraine, and Lee acknowledged this and put me on a pathway to have an assistance dog. This involved going to the Bravehound centre, which, at the time, was in a building behind the Erskine Hospital at Bishopton, near Glasgow, at regular intervals. Karla came with me, and together we got to know, over several weekends, a handsome male black Labrador. Rufus was a big lad and powerful. I have neck and shoulder problems and the assessor, Kate, quickly realised I wasn't suited to him. Then I was introduced to gorgeous Lynne – it was love at first sight! She reminded me of my sweet Bessie, only a white and cream version, rather than sleek black. She was a year old, still receiving training, but I was promised that I could soon take her home. So began what will be a lifelong relationship with Bravehound.

It was comforting being a part of a military community. We got there midmorning, did a bit of training with Kate, Kerry, Lorraine, Gwen, and June, or got further assessed, then broke off for a cooked meal, then more training. The meal was important to Karla and me – it was the first three course meal we'd had for months. We were still using the food bank, and this lunch helped nourish us with fresh vegetables and a fruit pudding. Our bellies were full for what felt like the first time since our savings ran out. Jimmy, another veteran, was the gifted cook along with Pamela and Elaine, two of the volunteers and Pamela still is a valued puppy socialiser. All three always ensured Karla and I ate well, and they have our grateful thanks.

We couldn't afford the petrol home and were always appreciative when Fiona or the dog trainers gave us fuel money from the valuable donations given to Bravehound. One week, a dog had eaten one of the twenty-pound notes from the trainer's bag! We had just enough fuel to get home and were praying hard all the way back. The fuel light was lit and dinging as we reached Aberdeenshire.

We were put up in the local Travelodge for the night. I was thankful, as I find driving tiring, as was the training – I had to use my brain power. I thought I knew how to handle a dog from Bouncer and Bessie's days, but training and handling an assistance dog is on another level. Fortunately, Lynne is a clever dog and responded well to the training and my handling.

Breakfast at the Travelodge was an opportunity to get well-fed again, and we were very aware that fundraisers were paying for it. My guilt soon kicked in, as did my self-worth regarding having an assistance dog when there are real military heroes who needed a Bravehound. There just aren't enough dogs to go round. I vowed to return the service by being the best advocate for Fiona and Gwyneth's charity as I could be. I wear the Bravehound t-shirt and fleece wherever I go, proudly showing off the Scotty dog emblem, and talk to people about the charity, although sometimes I can't face strangers. I hope Fiona doesn't mind.

I admire the way the charity is run. It's all for the welfare of the dog and veteran and carefully thought out and planned. I even had a sleepover with Lynne at the Travelodge, to test us both to ensure we were suitably matched. It felt strange taking her into the hotel; I was extremely nervous, but Lynne took it all in her stride, wearing her special working dog bib. I decided to step out of my comfort zone and walked her through a nearby shopping centre. My anxiety was at condition red, but with Lynne by my side, it lowered with each press of her muzzle against my hand. On my return to the hotel, I had to walk past the bar to get to the lifts. I was stopped by two big, burly workmen enjoying a pint after a hard day's work. They asked about Lynne and thanked me for my service. Then they offered to buy me a drink. It was humbling. No one has ever thanked me for my service before. They made me feel proud to be a veteran.

At bedtime, I moved her bed to the floor space by my side of the bed. It was reassuring to have her beside me. Then my nightmares came, and a strange thing happened. Lynne gently jumped up, nuzzled close into me, and awoke me from my terrors in a distinct way – she ever so gently put her nose to mine, then pushed her tongue into my mouth. Gawds! A technique not endorsed or taught by the Bravehound trainers. But it awoke me. I dried off my sweat with yesterday's t-shirt and settled down to sleep. But Lynne wouldn't leave my side. She must have still sensed my tension. Either that or the Travelodge mattress was more comfortable than hers! We both drifted off, cuddling, and spooning. That's when the second unusual thing happened. I had no further nightmares. My new best buddy had chased them away and had given me a warm, reassuring presence in my bed that lulled me into a deep sleep. I awoke refreshed.

We took her down to breakfast, and I rewarded her best behaviour with some of Travelodge's finest sausages. I knew the chef wouldn't have minded.

I reluctantly returned her to Julie, the puppy socialiser at Bravehound, and wanted to take her home immediately. Lynne, not Julie. I think Karla would have objected!

I didn't have long to wait to have her in her forever home. We'd passed the overnight test and Fiona and Kate, a caring member of the welfare team, dropped her off a few weeks later, along with a mountain of stuff that wouldn't have fitted in our car. We received two beds, a crate den, toys, brushes, bowls, leashes, food, training timetable sheets, dog worming tablets and flea treatment. All things I'd worried about not being able to afford.

Now that Lynne was in her forever home, another remarkable thing happened – my anxiety levels, normally at rocket level, plummeted throughout the day and only returned at night, as I put my head on my pillow in anticipation of the night terrors. Karla had banned Lynne from our bedroom at this stage. Lynne spent the nights in her den with her toys for company. I often wondered if my moans and screams woke her up.

It was great having my canine pal by my side. I took her into the garden, a place I usually avoided because of hammering on dustbin lids and other loud noises coming from a nearby house. I wore my noise-cancelling headphones and listened to a Big Finish Doctor Who drama while letting my white fantail doves fly off. Lynne sat patiently and watched them with me. She even sat and saw them safely plop into the sputnik one-way trap and into their shed for their seed breakfast. I took my coffee into the arbour, and she followed me, jumped up, and laid down with her head on my lap as we watched the starlings, blue tits and sparrows go from bird feeder to fat ball dispenser. It was lovely to feel so relaxed, and Lynne's warm muzzle was a reassuring presence. I didn't give a jot about the crazy neighbourhood antics.

The other advantage of having Lynne is she makes me get out of the house and walking. She needs exercise and though my knees and lower legs are painful, a stroll each day helps build up the muscles that support my aching joints. It's so lovely to be exploring the stunning village we live in. We have walks along the rugged coast, visit the nearby sandy beach, or tour around the lighthouse and harbour. Karla joins us for car runs to the nearby quarry and fields where Lynne can go off exploring and chase rabbits.

Having spent the first year of her life in the Glasgow area, Lynne wasn't used to the water. The first time we took her to Aberdeen beach, she went running off and then pelted away at the first wave that came gently over her. She's no brave hound! It would be a year of gentle coaxing to get her to swim in the sea. This was handy, as she loves to wallow in the muddy puddles and ditches on our moorland walks. A bath in the North Sea soon rids her of any mud and smells. Then it's a liberal spray of stinky dog dry shampoo and a good brush when we get home. I love the feel of her soft fur. It's so soothing and helps calm me.

I've a favourite spot near a castle where I used to take Bessie. Few people know of it and think it's a collection of large rocks. But beyond it is a shallow pool of constantly changing sea water, about chest height, but ideal as a swimming pool. Bessie was a flat-coated retriever, so instinctively took to the water when we moved from rural Suffolk to Aberdeenshire. We couldn't keep her out of the sea. One day, she even chased a seal far off into the sea. I returned home without her. No amount of recall could bring her back. The children went to school upset, thinking we'd never see her again. But she returned to the back door later that morning, waiting patiently as she drip-dried, an expression on her face saying, 'Where did you get to?' The children made a big fuss of her when they came home, red-eyed from crying.

We didn't have the same issue with Lynne. She wouldn't go near the natural swimming pool but backed away when I went near it with her. Instead, we sat on the nearby rocks, day after day. Then I dropped treats on the floor. Day by day, I dropped the treats nearer to the water. She gobbled them up, paws splayed on the shingle, ready to back away. But Lynne is highly motivated by food. She's a typical retriever who would happily eat all day. The treats soon got to the water's edge, then one day they were in the water, floating enticingly upon the surface. Lynne put a tentative paw in, reaching her snout as far as possible to get to them. The next day, I dropped them further in. To reach them, a reluctant Lynne had to put two paws in the water. Then we returned, and I threw the treats a foot further into the swimming pool and Lynne stepped in with all four paws and her belly getting wet to get those tasty Scooby snacks. Soon the tide carried them about six feet away and Lynne had to swim across to get them. Now she can wallow in the mud as much as she wants – she now swims across effortlessly to get those pesky floating and bobbing treats.

It was the same with all the training we did together; she was rewarded with a treat. Even if it meant she ate all day, she responded well to further training. I cut down on what I fed her at night so that her weight didn't balloon. Though this wasn't an issue thanks to the local wild rabbit population and their darting white tails. Lynne can't resist chasing them and trying to catch them soon burns the calories.

All the training Bravehound teaches us is reward and encouragement based. The positivity training creates a trust by the dog and helps bond the animal to the veteran through kindness. The bond between Lynne and me is unbreakable.

Each year, an assistance dog must undergo two tests before gaining their accreditation and in keeping it. The first is the public access test, which ensures that the dog behaves correctly in social situations, like a café or shop. The other is three specific tasks that benefit the owner of the dog.

Lynne has a naughty streak in her! How on earth was she going to pass the tests? When we visited the local cinema, she strained on the leash to reach other customers – and their popcorn! We tried to get around this by giving her a huge bone. She didn't finish it when the film ended, and we wanted to leave. She snarled at Karla and me when we tried to take it off her. When we eventually parted it from her, she squatted and did a pee on the carpet! I was mortified. The staff were polite about it and told us they have a special machine for such problems which are normally caused by young children. Not naughty Bravehounds! The charity was great though and thought of a super solution – Denise the Aberdeen dog whisperer.

Denise came to assess Lynne and would be my local dog trainer, or rather, human trainer. She laughed out loud when I told her about the revenge pee. Training an assistance dog is on a level far higher than a pet dog. She taught me so much and then I taught Lynne. We learnt the touch command, a useful checking in with each other tool where Lynne touches my hand with her nose. It's great for when she is distracted and needs to return her focus on me.

My shoulder pain was becoming unbearable because of Lynne pulling eagerly on the leash. Denise and I tried many tricks to get her to walk to heel, including saying out loud, 1, 2, 3, heel, and then feeding Lynne a treat. Fiona bought Lynne a special harness after Lynne had me off my feet when she chased a rabbit unexpectedly. This gave me greater control and eased some of the pulling on the leash. Denise and I tried feeding Lynne squirty cheese out of a tube as she walked beside me, then stinky meatballs. My pockets soon reeked.

Most beneficial of all was the under command where Lynne dives under my legs whenever I sit down. She's rewarded with a treat and is then fed at regular intervals to get her to stay there. It's handy for visiting the doctor, attending church on Remembrance Day and visits to the cinema.

She's been taught the cuddle and snuggle command for when I need comfort or her warm, reassuring presence during the awful flashbacks. She radiates heat and presses her belly and chest to mine, puts her front paws around my neck and snuggles into my neck. She soon chases away the images in my head or playing out in front of me and brings me back to the present.

The second command for my assistance test is to pick up for when I drop things. Stooping gives me no end of neck pain. I use a long-handled grabber at home, but now Lynne picks things up as soon as they fall, not only to help me, but for that all important treats. I have tubs of them scattered all around the house so she can be instantly rewarded.

Her third is round. She will walk all around me, clearing a space if shoppers get too close. I really dislike people being behind me. Lynne is happy to wander around me, getting a treat each time she passes my feet. No one gets between me and my dog when she's on a mission.

She has more commands, all taught by the Aberdeen dog whisperer. Denise runs Awesome Paws if you ever need help with your pooch. Other useful ones are give – handy for when we need to get something from Lynne. Leave is another important command, especially for the test. The examiner will set up a walk by food on the shop floor or will sit us down for coffee and drop a piece of cake. Lynne must leave them on command. Being food orientated, this took some training. In the end, Denise resorted to an obscure dog trainer technique where I have Lynne lying down and waiting (two more of her commands) and I had to walk around her humming, clapping my hands and hopping! I checked it wasn't the first of April.

This had to be done indoors, in the garden, and then in the local sports field. The village must have thought they had a new idiot! But it worked. Lynne now has a strong leave command.

On the day of the test, we tired Lynne out with a long walk followed by lots of chasing her ball around a field. Then we met Doctor Rob, our examiner, at a garden centre. He has a PhD in dog training, so knows his stuff. He's also a fellow army veteran, so knows about PTSD. He put me at ease instantly with his relaxing manner. Lynne walked beautifully to heel around the shop. She left the food spilt deliberately along the dog food aisle. Rob even forgave her for jumping up on him halfway through the test. Oops! She performed lots of touch commands. She picked up a fallen object, cuddled, and snuggled me and passed with flying colours. I was as surprised as Karla was. Our naughty madam is now a fully accredited assistance dog and comes with me wherever I go. Mind you, I don't think she was impressed at being at the doctor's when I needed a prostate exam. I wasn't impressed either! I shall speak of that no more, other than to say that Lynne laid down and chomped on a chew while the doctor's finger boldly went where none have gone before.

She still has her naughty moments, like jumping onto a restaurant table to nick a paper napkin. She keeps me entertained and all the training and keeping her well behaved has been a great distraction from my PTSD and stops my mind wandering back to the past. She's given me a reason to get up in the morning, rather than wallowing in bed in a sea of misery. She has helped heal my grief, and though I have bad days where I really miss my son and despair at what happened to him, Lynne soon picks up my mood with her antics.

I will always be indebted to Bravehound for their support, in picking me up from my bootstraps and getting me back on my feet. Lynne sits or lies by my desk now that I am back to full-time writing again. I get great comfort from knowing that readers enjoy my novels. I feel a useful part of society again. All because I have Lynne walking by me, every step of the way. Fiona and her team are my guardian angels.

I like to say yes to everything Fiona asks me to do, no matter if it is out of my comfort zone. I agreed to go to the Glasgow dog show, to help run a stall promoting Bravehound. It was loud! Stimuli was firing at me in all directions. Music blared from speakers, interspersed by a shouting host. There was the chatter and hum of conversations. My relaxation techniques were put through the wringer on those two days. But I managed it, with Lynne by my side. I spoke to strangers about my PTSD and how Bravehound supports me and how my life has been changed for the better. It pleased me to see them reach for the donation tin. Being a charity, these donations are vital for Bravehound to continue their important work. I hope I sell lots of copies of this book, because profits are being split amongst the charities that helped Abigail, Karla, and me and Bravehound is a big part of that.

Lynne proved once more that she has a naughty streak and was a bit of a chancer. A toddler was making a beeline for Lynne, arm stretched out, ready to give her a stroke. But in his other hand was a sausage roll. Crafty Lynne leant into the stroke, allowed the toddler to clap her, then ever so gently took the proffered meaty delight out of his other hand and swallowed it whole. The dad burst out laughing and the child looked stunned. But not as shocked as Fiona, who'd seen the whole thing. Oops! My secret was out, and she now knew Lynne was the naughtiest Bravehound, the wee chancer! The dad wouldn't take any money for a new sausage roll and went off chuckling while his son looked at his empty hand, trying to work out the magic disappearing trick. Well, dogs will be dogs, no matter how much training they receive.

There was one night that I felt I let Fiona down. It was an open night promoting Bravehound. The press was there, and I hadn't realised that a photographer would be there too. With his flash. One of my triggers. Boom – I was right back in the mortuary. Unwanted images were playing around my head like a videotape. The flashing continued. I couldn't speak. I was frozen to the spot. Lynne was straight on me, nudging, cuddling, and snuggling. Then Karla and one volunteer led me to safety, away from the crowds and the flash photography. I felt I had let Fiona and the team badly down. I should have been out there answering questions from the guests, showing them how much Lynne was helping me. She had, though. She'd recognised I was in trouble, alerting Karla and the volunteer that I was having flashbacks and needed to get somewhere quiet.

Most of the Bravehounds are named after recipients of the Dickens medal. An honour that is presented to those heroic animals who bravely helped win us the World Wars. Some get named after other special people, and so it is for Lynne. A kind husband, (Bernard), his son, (Christopher) and daughter, (Bernadette), donated Lynne after they lost their dear wife and mother. Her name was Lynne. Her family follows Lynne on social media, and I was touched one day when they contacted me to say how loving their mother was and that they could see that her spirit lives on in my dear Lynne. It was emotional reading their messages and I hope we do her memory proud. Their generosity in their time of loss has helped heal my grief and aided me in learning to live with the debilitating effects of military PTSD. I will always be indebted to them.

I love her gorgeous name. We are so bonded that Karla nicknames her The Mistress! She's got other names for her when she is naughty! Lynne and I call Karla the Other Woman! I even said this on STV News when they did a story about Lynne and me. We are rarely parted, just when I go to the toilet – I must draw the line somewhere. Even then, Lynne waits patiently outside for me.

This has been a long chapter, the biggest in this book. It shows just what a large part of my life Lynne has become, all thanks to the benevolence of the family who donated her and Fiona and her team.

I mentioned puppy socialisers. They play a huge part in getting the dogs ready for veterans. They have them from about twelve weeks and take them into their homes and families and bring them up in normal conditions until they are ready to be re-homed to veterans. It must be a big wrench to give them up. But it must also be rewarding work. They get given homework from Al, Kerry, Gwen, and June, the dog trainers. Applicants to be a puppy socialiser are always welcome.

We made some great friendships amongst trainers like Lorraine and Kate, who also looked after the welfare of us veterans. A sweet teenager, Fiona, volunteered at the centre and enjoyed bathing the Bravehounds and learning about PTSD. She wrote an informative piece about it for her school project and showed a deep understanding of the effects of PTSD. Her mum Elaine, also a veteran, came with her and we enjoy their company. It's been lovely to see Fiona bloom into a lovely young woman. Karla and I had a meal at their farmhouse and met their flat-coated retriever, a handsome lad called Zeus. Karla painted a stunning portrait of him for Elaine and one for Fiona's Jack Russell, Sky. I think her best pet portrait was of Gwyneth. It's simply stunning and you could almost reach out and pet it. I drop hints to Karla each birthday and Christmas for a portrait of Lynne.

If you are a veteran with mental health issues, please consider applying for a Bravehound when their application process is open or foster a dog from your local re-homing centre or buy a puppy from a reputable breeder. The same if you are a grieving parent or sibling. Consider what pet you could have to provide comfort and a focus for your day. I still have my doves and love watching them fly around. I used to have chickens, and they had character and loved sitting on my lap in the arbour. Each had their own personalities. If you are gaining comfort and help from this book, or are enjoying reading about Lynne and me, please consider leaving a donation at Bravehound to help more veterans. Visit their website at www.bravehound.co.uk.

CHAPTER 23:

TRIGGERS

Every veteran will have had a unique experience during their service life. I think myself lucky in not having gone on active service. I had, however, postings to Belize and Cyprus where there was no 999. I formed part of the emergency response teams. It was a wake -up call to the real service life. Prior to then, it was clinical and well-controlled in hospitals in Aldershot, Woolwich, and Maidstone. But as part of the Field Surgical Team and manning the casualty department, I saw what happens when things go violently wrong. I have seen a fair amount of training accidents and vehicle and aircraft crashes. These travel at high speeds, particularly the planes, and when they crash, it is devastating.

I've seen various wounds, burns, amputations, and limb breaks. I've witnessed a lot of death. Far too much. When Angus took his life, the traumas I've been part of in the past latched onto my personal trauma and resulted in my military PTSD escalating until it was out of control. I have certain triggers that cause me to have flashbacks and nightmares. Some I can explain, others seem illogical.

Anyone who has been in combat will have different triggers. The same goes for other nurses. Those who have lost a relative to suicide will also have specific triggers. I do.

In this chapter, I'll explain mine as best as I can. If it isn't too upsetting, I think you will benefit from making a list of your PTSD triggers and sharing them with your loved ones and healthcare professionals. It will help to discuss these with a psychologist.

I first found that flash photography sets off flashbacks when attending a Burns supper. I was looking forward to a night of Robert Burns' poetry and haggis, neeps, and tatties, though I felt daunted by the crowds. It was a large gathering, and I was there as part of my work, covering the event for my website, www.aboutaberdeen.com — it was an attempt at the Guinness World Record for the largest Burns Supper. A photographer was there with a state-of-the-art camera, taking pictures to sell to the guests. He had a bright flash, and we had to walk past him to get to our table. Having my picture taken is something I have never been comfortable with. I didn't know why until that night. I'd been newly diagnosed with military PTSD and was learning about the condition and what treatments I needed. I was soon to understand why I hated the camera so much; the flashing set off a chain of events in my head. I was back at the mortuary, helping move the Tornado jets pilot and navigator bodies so that the crash investigator team could take photographs for their inquiry. There was still so much blood, and the state of the bodies was indescribable. I've kept describing the horrific injuries to a minimum in this book out of respect to them and their families.

Blood is another trigger of mine and fortunately I don't see a lot of it these days. I'm not like Doc Martin in the ITV programme staring Martin Clunes. I'm fine with tiny amounts, it's the pools of it that trigger me. It's fortunate that I no longer work as a nurse. It's left me a bit OCD about handwashing and keeping my arms clean. I recently painted the sheds cedar red and that'll be a colour I'll no longer buy. When it dried on my hands, it resembled dried blood too much and it led to much scrubbing, so much so that my hands were chapped for weeks. The amount of blood I had to walk through to get to the bodies in the back of the rescue chopper was unbelievable. The stench has never truly left my nostrils. I've seen oesophageal varices burst and bleed out and compound fractures and traumatic amputations, and these were nothing compared to the amount lost because of the multiple injuries suffered by the jet crew. I had to help pick them up and carry them. My uniform had to be destroyed.

It took me a while to work out why loud noises, especially loud bangs that seemed to come from the house wall, unnerved me and made me hyperalert and anxious. This isn't a fleeting anxiety, but a crushing heavy weight upon my chest that causes pain, makes me hyperventilate and can lead me to be uneasy for days after. They remind me of the sound of the aircraft crashing. It was heard around the airbase, not just at the hospital. I can only imagine what combat must have been like for my fellow veterans. Now loud bangs take me right back to running to the helipad, watching the rescue helicopter land, and seeing the loadmaster, covered in blood, slicing his finger across his throat. Then I'm back there, stepping into the chopper, sliding in the blood, and picking up the bodies. This was nothing like a clinically clean death on a hospital bed. It was the worst of training exercises gone wrong. Worse than any road traffic accident or burns victim. I now wear noise-cancelling headphones as much as possible. They block out unexpected bangs.

Helicopters are my nemesis. They bring back some terrible memories and with them unwanted flashbacks. Here in the North East of Scotland, the biggest employers are still oil rigs and fishing. I live under the flight path for the choppers as they ferry the workers from Dyce Airport to the rigs. There are also the search helicopters when ships or walkers are in trouble along the coast. As if these weren't enough triggers, the police helicopters use our coastline as a training area. The noise-cancelling headphones from Help for Heroes have been a lifeline and block out most of the rotor noises. If I listen to Big Finish audio dramas, then I don't hear the blades and engines at all. Spaceships and Daleks sound nothing like a landing helicopter bringing home bodies. Whenever I have been to helicopters in my military career, they have never brought good news and the sights and what I had to do haunt me. They also inhabit my nightmares, and I try to avoid seeing and hearing them. But you'd be surprised how often helicopters pop up on TV, on radio plays and at the cinema. Karla vets most things for me and I'm usually a few days behind on current TV, but the cinema has been the worst for my anxiety. The sound is stereo, and the vision is too close. If you had me on a heart monitor, my pulse and blood pressure would be sky high and the comedown would take hours, sometimes days. Even in the most romantic of comedies, one always seems to slip in. My favourites are pre-1950s set films and I adore musicals and the old black and white films on the telly. Though I'm not sure Lynne enjoys me singing along to them.

I can no longer enjoy walks at Hazlehead Park in Aberdeen. The choppers are too near the ground as they fly to nearby Dyce Airport.

It's the same for flights from Aberdeen Airport. The sight and sounds of helicopters as we board a plane are too much for me. Having Lynne is the perfect excuse not to holiday abroad.

When Karla had her spectacular fight with the German bunker during our holiday in Jersey, she was taken to the local hospital in an ambulance. The paramedics were super and cared for her brilliantly. They told me to accompany them.

I've been in a few ambulances in my time, but as a nurse and medic, not a relative. Seeing the stretchers and equipment brought back a flood of emotions, memories, and flashbacks. I had a real fight on my hands that night, and the paramedic must have wondered why I was so quiet. I was just managing to hold on to reality during the drive to Casualty. I'm glad to say that I haven't been in another ambulance since. I hope it's a long time until the next one. No more night manoeuvres for Karla!

This one I found unusual, but I get highly anxious when people block my exit from a room or building. Wherever I go, I need to know how quickly I can leave and where each exit is and alternative ways out.

Even something as simple as Karla standing in the kitchen doorway, writing on the calendar makes me edgy. We used to have fights about locating it somewhere else. I've given up and try to relax, but it's a struggle.

Another example was at the funeral of a friend. The pub where the wake was held was heaving, and I tried to get out from the crowds, but another friend, who I hadn't seen for a while, suddenly popped out of nowhere and innocently barred my way. He tried to engage me in conversation, but I barged past him in my frantic need to get out. I know it was rude and I hope he forgives me. I know I would have coped better if I had Lynne with me, but this was a pre-Bravehound time.

It took me a long time to understand my actions and acute anxiety and I think it stems from being shut in with the dead Tornado crew and not being able to get out of the ambulance. It was a feeling of powerlessness and being trapped.

Mortuaries are easily explained as a trigger and viewing Angus at the police morgue was the primary catalyst for my military PTSD exploding in my head. My anxiety about losing Abigail sometimes gets too much for me, too, and I go for a swift walk with Lynne to help calm me. I feel the trees as I walk past them, smell blossom, and try to get in touch with nature to calm me. When she went bungee jumping, a few months ago, I was on condition red, until I knew she was all right.

I so wanted to break down that glass screen and hold my son, but when there is a death by suicide, the police treat the body as a crime exhibit or scene and it seems cruel to not allow families to hold their loved one's hand, stroke their face and embrace them. It delays the healing process not being able to do these simple acts.

I pray there will be the natural order of things and I won't ever see Abigail the way we last saw our dear son.

Sometimes, when our family finances are taking a hit, I say to Karla that perhaps I should give up writing and go back to nursing. She rolls her eyes and says a sarcastic, 'Yeah, right?' We both know that I could never go back to a caring profession. I could not cope with more traumas, the dying, and the dead.

The NHS psychologist who treated me said it correctly when I spoke about retraining as a grief counsellor. She told me I've had my share of trauma and it wouldn't be fair for me to have to cope with other people's traumas. Last year I applied to be a befriender at The Compassionate Friends, but the trainer of the two-day course was allergic to dogs, and I couldn't bear to be parted from Lynne. I hadn't the heart to explain she is an assistance dog, and he was breaking the law by not allowing me to take her. It's a shame. I think I would have been good at that, and I would have brought some comfort to grieving mothers, fathers, and siblings in my area. It's the quiet life for me now. No more dramas.

The psychologist politely told me off when she learned I was watching as many TV programmes and films with helicopters in them as possible and looking at pictures of them online to desensitise myself to them. It didn't work, and she was right to tell me off. Please don't try this at home!

It's the same for you, perhaps? If you have served your country, accept that you can't be expected to go into battle again. If you have loved and lost, then pray that you'll never experience a deep loss again. Grief changes our brains and outlooks. I try to lighten the load of the few people I meet with a cheery conversation and not add to their burden. I have a maudlin perspective now and must fight the black dog that is depression. I have the added burden of PTSD and just want to be alone. I spend the day avoiding triggers, managing my anxiety and flashbacks, and coping with nightmares. I'm so glad I have Lynne by my side in this war.

I don't go to places where there may be sizeable crowds, but sometimes Karla drags me to days out like the zoo. We usually go to such places during school terms to avoid large gatherings of people. I've been social distancing for years, prior to Covid. However, we can't control large groups of school children on a trip or parents with their pre-school children. I learnt on one such trip that the sound of crying children gives me a rush of emotions regarding Angus. I can't get on top of it and end up crying. In despair at my loss, but also knowing the physical and emotional pain that was inflicted on Angus during the crime, and for a year after when he bravely faced his demons alone.

I also get triggered when I hear people chastise a child roughly. It not only sparks unpleasant memories of my childhood, but I want to stop the scolding and tell the perpetrator that life is so fleeting, and love should be the way to teach children. I so admire Bravehound and the trainers for teaching positivity to train our dogs. It creates a greater respect and trust from the dog and strengthens our bonds. Be kind to your children and tell them and others that you love them because one day you won't be able to.

Share that list of triggers with those who are close to you. Work out how to avoid as many as possible. It isn't cowardice, it's common sense. You deserve some peace in your life and any way you can avoid flashbacks, stress and anxiety is a good thing.

CHAPTER 24:

ANGER

I've had to work hard in taming my anger. Developing PTSD was a confusing and frightening time. I was seeing corpses and body parts that I knew weren't there, but there they were, right in front of me. I could smell that sharp tang of blood or the roasting of flesh. Odours that are never forgotten once experienced. I could reach out and pick them up again. Only I didn't want to, never again. I shouted and screamed in protest. To my shame, I punched through a door and smashed a dining room chair against the floor until it shattered. My mind couldn't take in what I was seeing, and I needed to vent.

There was also the terrible rage against the man who committed the despicable crime against Angus, and I blamed him entirely for his suicide. Thank heavens we checked his bin and found his first draft suicide letter. I was angry at the police for not telling us there were, in fact, letters left by him before he took his life. I was angry that they wiped the data from his phone and laptop before returning them to us. We needed answers, and I yearned to get my hands on the perpetrator. I would have torn his heart out, like he has for Abigail, Karla, and I. Despite my aching knees and lower legs, I would go for furious walks, forcing myself to go faster and get my pulse racing. I needed to excise this cancer in my mind.

There was never anger at Angus for taking his life, though some reading this book and have been affected by suicide can find themselves in this emotional state. And that's fine. So long as you work through it with a professional, like a counsellor or psychologist. Anger is strength sapping. My emotion in relation to Angus was despair. I felt I'd let him down. There was a deep sadness. I cried lots. I went to cliffs, stood on the edge, and screamed. These were base, carnal, savage screams of rage. It helped. Then I would contemplate throwing myself off because I couldn't cope with my grief and PTSD. Not having a peaceful home didn't help. I needed to sit without some despicable banging on walls day and night. That's why I snapped and shouted in rage at the person who was distressing Abigail on the day of Angus's funeral by banging a ladder outside her bedroom window for hours. Like many a veteran with PTSD, I got in trouble with the police. Months later, I was seen by the court officials and my anger had subsided and they noted that though their usual paths would have been to send me on an anger management course, they couldn't see any in me. I'd entered a deep depression and instead they sent me to Combat Stress, not that they helped me either. Thank heaven for the NHS and my amazing GP and psychologist and then Bravehound.

Anger has been prominent in my childhood. I thought it was normal to be beaten with fists by your mother and father. I thought it was normal to have a belt taken to you. But it isn't. My psychologist helped me see that. It was abuse. I remember my childhood being happy until I was seven. Then my father left home for a few weeks. Along with my older brother, we were sent to a flat in Ruthrieston, near to where we lived in Garthdee, Aberdeen. The door was opened by a gracious lady, and we went in and gave dad a message from mum that he was to come home. I never learned who the lady was, but the beatings and anger started soon after he came home.

The first I can still vividly remember was from my mother. I left for school, and she told me to come back into the house. Innocently, I turned back from the gate and went to her. She ushered me inside, closed the door and rained fists down upon my shocked body. This went on for about a minute. I guess she tired herself out as I was crouched down, innocently protecting my face. I made a bolt for the door and cried all the way to school. My crime? I had forgotten my playtime orange and my mother had not wanted the school to think she hadn't provided me with food.

I learned from an early age to keep out of arm's length from my parents. Even if I was doing something as innocent as reading a book, they would come and clout me over the head. I received the belt across my back or bottom for the slightest misdemeanour. I was slippered too, though by this time that didn't hurt as much as the fists or belt. This went on until I left school, or rather was told to get a job and stop wasting time on education. I so wanted to attain A levels, or Highers as they were called here in Scotland. I yearned to go to university and better myself.

I took the first job the Job Centre offered me. It was as a sales assistant at Millets on Union Street, Aberdeen. I knew a little about tents and sleeping bags from my time as a Scout, though I'd left them a few years earlier because I could no longer pay for the weekly subs nor afford the cost of camping trips and the equipment. My parents didn't support me. I had to work doing two paper rounds and selling cream and bacon door to door on a Saturday morning. I also sold toffee in the evenings. I worked hard. I needed to so that I could buy my school uniforms and even food. I was always hungry and food at home was scarce. I recall the indignation of having a ripped hole in the only pair of school trousers I had. It flapped whenever I moved. Mum wouldn't sew them up, let alone wash them. Nor my underpants. It took me months to save up for a fresh pair. And I stank of urine. My school mates would move their chair away from me and tease me. I have no friends from my school days.

Once the beatings started, I began wetting the bed. There was more anger at the smells and extra bedding and pyjama washing, though most times I had to return to the wet bed. Mum told my brother to go around the primary school telling everyone I wet the bed. This resulted in more teasing, and I have no pals from my primary school days either. I think that's why I'm so fastidious about wearing clean clothes each day and having the bedding stripped frequently.

I was told by the teacher that I would soon see someone for an assessment. I think it was a nurse who came to the school. When I told my mum, she drilled it into me I was to say I was happy at home. I was anything but. It was a miserable childhood and my psychologist called it neglect when I talked about it decades later. I had nothing to compare it to as I was rarely invited to friend's houses and even then, mum would deny me permission. I seldom had a friend around to the house. My mum said I wasn't to invite anyone over as they might steal something. I remember being pals with Gregory. His mum was lovely, and she invited me in to watch Wimbledon with them and to listen to The Police music with Gregory. When mum found out, she made me tell Gregory that I wasn't to be his friend anymore. It broke my heart; I enjoyed having a friend.

I had friends on the same street though, and we played outside, never in our home. I guess they didn't mind my smell being outside. We would play football and cricket on the nearby primary school grounds. I think they moved away by the time I went to secondary school, as I can't recall seeing them beyond this time.

My father soon tired of me being at home at sixteen. I'd tried to gain entry as a police officer cadet but failed the interviews. I passed academically, but I was a quiet child – I had to be, otherwise I'd get a clout or beating. I wouldn't have been suited for the role. He marched me first to the Royal Air Force and then to the Royal Navy recruiting offices. I failed to gain entry at my immature age. Then he took me to the army recruiting offices, who welcomed me with open arms. Except I knew I didn't want to kill anyone, and dad wanted me to join the local infantry regiment, The Gordon Highlanders. Instead, I read the pamphlets the army sergeant gave me and requested to join the Royal Army Medical Corps as a medic. I passed and was soon to be sent to Keogh Barracks for basic training at the tender age of seventeen. I was the youngest recruit in our intake.

The weeks prior to my overnight train from Aberdeen to Ash Vale, my dad would pin me to the floor and rain blows down on me, shouting 'You can't take it!' I can't explain this behaviour. Perhaps he thought he was toughening me up. As it was, basic training was a breeze compared to being at home. I had clean clothes, could shower, or bathe each day, sometimes twice if we had a strenuous boot run along the muddy fields. Our sergeant loved to get us doing press-ups in ditches! I didn't even complain about stretcher races in Mytchett Lake – it all got me clean. I no longer smelled. All I needed was to change my underpants each day and have a shower or bath. Even the shouting drill sergeant and training centre corporals were pussy cats compared to my parents. The only problem was leave. I had nowhere to go. During weekend passes, my pals all went home. I stayed at the empty barracks rooms by myself and felt ever so alone. The corporals noted I hadn't requested a train pass and twigged. I was made to go home for the next long weekends.

Things had changed. I was taller and broader thanks to three square meals a day. I was also more confident, thanks to the military training. Dad and Mum kept their fists and shouting to themselves. Perhaps they feared retaliation now that I'd had unarmed combat training. That physical training instructor terrified us recruits! But he taught us some back street fighting techniques, even though we were supposed to be non-armed combatants.

I vowed not to get angry with any children I may have, and I hope I was a better father to Angus and Abigail than mine was. He was a poor example of a parent and I showed as much love to my children as I could get away with, without embarrassing them!

Lynne has been a great soother to my soul, and I rarely get angry now. She did witness one outburst, after a bad flashback, soon after she came to her forever home. She looked in fear of me, ears pinned back, and she came and snuggled into me until I calmed down. She's a clever girl and keeps me grounded.

Identify the anger in yourself, talk it over with those most affected, like your partner, children, or friends. Try to identify its source and see how you can avoid anger triggers. Then find an outlet for your anger, like running, going to the gym, meditation, or yoga. Or screaming - just make sure it's in an isolated area or in a pillow so you don't distress others. The coping techniques I talk about later will help with your anger.

CHAPTER 25:

DENIAL

The first battle to win in the war with PTSD and grief is denial. Despite a GP, counsellor, the court system, Combat Stress psychiatric nurse and an NHS psychologist telling me I clearly had PTSD, I shook my head each time and said it was grief. How wrong was I! I had both. Do yourself a big favour and learn from my mistake and accept your diagnosis. It'll help you in the long-run and is far healthier.

When the police sat us down in our lounge and told us Angus had taken his own life, we shook our heads and said no. We explained he had everything to live for. He had his own flat, a responsible job with a defined career pathway, a good wage and lots of friends. He came from a loving home. His relationship with Abigail was the tightest brother and sister bond I've ever seen. He seemed happy and healthy when we saw him last. We questioned if it was the right address and the younger police officer said yes and that he knew Angus from having to take statements at McDonald's when they had unruly customers or a spate of thefts in the staff lockers. It wasn't until we saw him at the police mortuary did our hearts sink and tears start. The numbness stayed for months.

I was in the army during the 1980s and 90s. We received no training about PTSD, not even during my general nurse training. I spent the psychiatric block on a general ward – it was a new curriculum, and we were expected to learn about the mental health needs of surgical patients. I don't recall even hearing about PTSD amongst my fellow medics and nurses, though I'm sure some must have had it. I hope things have changed for the modern military. It was only as my EMDR treatment progressed did I realise that I truly had military PTSD and from seeing Angus at the police mortuary.

Sometimes I relapse and question with Karla if the medical professionals may have got it wrong as I feel okay these days. She rolls her eyes and says something sarcastic back and reminds me of my abnormal feelings and nightmares. Lynne keeps me on the straight and narrow. I'd be lost without her. She tames my anxiety and chases away my flashbacks and nightmares. Her warm body against mine is so reassuring. Thank you, Lee, for teaching her the cuddle command. It is invaluable.

Try to rid yourself of your denial and face reality, no matter how painful it is. Help is available. As are coping techniques.

CHAPTER 26:

FLASHBACKS

My first flashback was about two weeks after the Tornado crash. A General was visiting the hospital in Cyprus and arrived by helicopter. I was coming off shift and my car was parked in the staff car park next to the helipad. It was like a bomb had been thrown into my head. I felt dizzy, was hyperventilating, and was in sheer panic. I had returned there, in the back of the helicopter, lifting out the dead crew. I saw their wounds, could smell, and see the blood. My hands were clean. I had just had a shower in the changing rooms. But I could see my hands and body were covered in another's blood. I ran to the car, neglecting to salute to the General as he made his way to the hospital gardens where Matron and the Commanding Officer were stood in a line along with the ward Sisters and invited staff. I don't know how I got home, but I did. I headed straight to the shower, then to the bay with Bouncer to make sense of what I experienced.

My bicycle was getting a repair in the local bike shop, it was rare for me to drive to the hospital. I loved the exercise. I made sure never to drive to work again, nor go near the staff car park and the helipad.

Night shift was always a quiet time. Most of the patients were military or were their family members. They were young and were in for only one ailment or operation, so there was no polypharmacy or complications because of diabetes, etc. They mostly cared for themselves, with a little help from us nurses. In the early hours, I went to the hospital library and looked through journals for articles on PTSD. There was no internet in 1994 for us military. PCs were being introduced, and I was getting trained in Word, with the helpful paperclip icon, remember him?

I read the symptoms and ticked them off in my head. But I was still convinced only combat military personnel developed PTSD, and only years after an event. I tried to soldier on as best as I could and nurse to the best of my ability. But I couldn't avoid the mortuary, blood, ambulances, and the inevitable helicopters. I turned to whisky to help me cope. I feigned an interest in malts, so the drinks cabinet had lots of bottles so that I could drink a good amount without Karla noticing. I shopped whilst she was busy with the children and added a bottle with the bread and vegetables. I pretended I needed extra beer because I was so thirsty in the Cypriot heat.

I hung onto reality as best as I could. When the nightmares started, I would get up and walk Bouncer. Years later, it would be Bessie, and now my beautiful Lynne.

It was a terrifying, bewildering time, and once my posting to Cyprus was over, I resigned from the army. I could no longer cope with the trauma.

Now I breathe through the flashbacks or hang onto Lynne for dear life. I took the cuddle command a stage further and taught her the snuggle command, where she rests her muzzle deep into my neck. I bury my face in her soft neck and slowly stroke her fur to calm me. She has a distinctive smell. I love it. I inhale deeply and slowly exhale until I am grounded in the present. It's one of several coping techniques. Medication helps too, especially the Pregabalin, particularly when I was prescribed the highest dosages, twice a day.

I know some veterans act out flashback scenes as if they are reliving moments of combat. I don't think I do this unless Karla hasn't told me in case it upsets me. I've heard from others that they shout out orders, act out putting on their helmet, webbing, picking up and aiming a rifle. It must be equally terrifying to see. I'm so glad I never saw combat. A huge respect to those who did.

Anyone can develop PTSD and develop flashbacks. Sexual abuse survivors, accident survivors and even those whose job it is to watch videos of ghastly crimes. The list is endless and includes those who found their relative or friend dead by suicide. I still get flashbacks to seeing Angus dead in the police mortuary, lying under the purple blanket, his face mottled. I wish I could get beyond the glass and hold him. But I will never see him again, other than in these visions. They do not bring any comfort and I try to remember him during happier times.

Find your own coping strategy, accept professional help, accept your diagnosis of PTSD, and ride out those flashbacks as best you can. Avoid your triggers wherever possible.

CHAPTER 27:

ANXIETY

Unless you've experienced anxiety, I don't think most people really appreciate just how debilitating it can be. Mine is like a heavy weight has been thudded against my chest, then pressed further in. It can stay for hours, sometimes days. I also get pain radiating through to my back and between my shoulder blades. I've had to go to the local A&E and had cardiac tests when I first developed anxiety. If I hear a loud bang, or any of the other triggers, it's an instant anxiety attack, and it takes a long time to shrug them off. Sometimes weeks. I go to sleep feeling anxious until my medication drifts me off. Then I wake with anxiety. It's a horrible feeling that I cannot always control, but I have coping mechanisms, and Lynne now helps tremendously. I call her my miracle dog. Karla calls her something else when Lynne is being mischievous!

Breathing exercises help me with the hyperventilating and I've other techniques to get me and keep me calm. Lynne is my best medication for anxiety, though antidepressants, like mirtazapine at its highest dose, is the best for me. I've tried others through prescription and over-the-counter drugs, but none worked for me. I've heard of veterans who smoke weed to help with their anxiety, though I wouldn't recommend this as it may cause brain damage and lead to paranoia in later life. It can also cause psychotic illnesses like schizophrenia. You've enough mental health issues going on, please don't add to them.

I used to think that anxiety was something old ladies got, or someone worrying about an exam. How little I knew! It's devastating and should never be underplayed. It can affect relationships, work, and social life. It can ruin your mental and physical health. In my case, I now have gastric problems because of my body's natural reaction in releasing chemicals to cope with my anxiety.

It makes me want to stay at home, where I feel safe, and not have to interact with people. Though this probably isn't healthy either. I like my company and the safety of wearing my headphones and being in control of what podcasts I listen to and the background noises I hear.

Anxiety is common amongst people trying to live with PTSD. Triggers bring us back to memories and events we'd rather not relive, but do. Military PTSD is no stranger to anxiety, nor is it for those living with grief.

A lot of my anxiety centres around Abigail and her safety. Losing a child is devastating and affects you for life. But you can learn to live a new way of life and I need to accept that Angus and Abigail were and are free to make their own choices. Angus carefully thought through his suicide, even down to leaving an e-mail to The Samaritans to say by the time they read it he would be dead and could they send the police to deal with his body. I've reluctantly had to accept it as his free choice to end his suffering.

I can't do much against my anxiety, flashbacks, and nightmares, other than take the medicine and enjoy my life with Lynne. The years between dogs were anxiety-ridden and I don't want to go back there. I hope Lynne and I have many more years together. She gives the best cuddles.

My anxiety has been diagnosed as General Anxiety Disorder, GAD.

Talk openly with your mental health professional or family about your anxiety and fears. Try to avoid the triggers you've identified earlier.

Bring rationale to your mind and look at things in a more positive frame of mind. A useful exercise is to write, or type into your phone notes or laptop document, each evening, three things that you were grateful for that day. Research has shown that those who do this lead happier, anxiety free lives and that it can change your brain from depression to a positive outlook.

A friend gifted me a Good News jar. I slip my pieces of paper into this. As an example, today I was grateful to have had a stroll with Lynne to the nearby sports field, I read a chapter of my favourite author, Gerald Seymour's latest novel, and I watched a Sylvester Stallone film I've never seen before, and it had no helicopters in it!

CHAPTER 28:

DEPRESSION

Anxiety did not come alone; it brought an unwelcome friend called depression. This isn't just a low mood, it is stay in bed, curl up in a ball depression. It is seeing grey, not colour. It is standing on a cliff, about to hurl myself off, depression.

I can understand why Winston Churchill called his depression the black dog. It felt to me that a black cloud had descended upon my life. I barely functioned. I ate all the wrong things. I didn't partake in my usual hobbies and interests. I only got out of bed when I really had to, and even that was a struggle. If it wasn't for my white fantail doves needing fed, I would never have gone outside. As it was, I would just go to the back garden and then inside. The gardening was neglected, our housework and décor were neglected. As was my appearance. I barely shaved and hated visits to the barber. Piles of my beloved Doctor Who Magazine lay in my study unread for two years, until we were offered free holidays and I slipped some into my suitcase.

I think I worried my GP, counsellor, and psychologist. I terrified Karla. Fortunately, all three health professionals healed me through talking therapy, EMDR, and medication. And then Bravehound accepted me, and I got my sweet Lynne – the best medicine for my depression. I saw colour again. I went further than the back garden.

We enjoy walks in various places and when I go to feed my birds, Lynne comes with me and loves to watch them and the wild birds too. She's splendid company and rarely leaves my side. She is my protector. Today she sat patiently watching a magpie at the fat ball feeder. I think in envy, she so loves a fat ball if I accidentally drop one. Woof, and it's got. I've never seen her move so fast. It gets gobbled faster than I can utter the leave command. I don't mind – she's much better behaved in cafes and restaurants. Honest!

Losing Angus to suicide was catastrophic. It felt like the end of my life. If I didn't have Abigail, I would have ended my life. My GP called her my protective factor. The thing that stopped me from ending my life. Abigail, though now a young lady, needs her dad. And I'd made a promise to myself years ago to be the best dad I could. I had to find a way through this pain, depression, anxiety, panic attacks, nightmares, and flashbacks. No matter how painful it was for me, and it was for about three years. It still is, sometimes. But I promise you, if I can live through the suicide of my son and developing PTSD, you can too. Keep reading this book.

My diagnosis was clinical depression, as well as General Anxiety Disorder and Post Traumatic Stress Disorder – a triple-whammy. But help was available. Combat Stress, Poppy Scotland, The Royal British Legion, my Regimental Association, and the other charities may have neglected to help me, but others did. They will always have my grateful thanks and support.

I still take my medications at the higher strengths. They keep me staying positive and less gloomy. They help me function during the day. I'm back to work. We are slowly paying off our debts, and I take time to enjoy life again, especially with Lynne. My GP reaches out to me periodically to make sure I'm on the straight and narrow and I no longer need therapy. Life can be sweet again after losing a child and developing PTSD. It just takes time. I took one day at a time.

Consider a visit to your GP and talk about your possible depression and treatment paths, be they talking therapies or medication.

CHAPTER 29:

SEASONAL AFFECTIVE DISORDER

I don't have Seasonal Affective Disorder, but Karla does. It's appropriately abbreviated to SAD, and that is what it makes you. It typically hits in October for her and her moods dip, she sleeps more during the day, feels lethargic, and her depression gets worse than mine. She will stay in bed for a long time, will need encouragement to do activities like shower or change her clothes and even eat properly. Her sleep pattern will become disrupted. All her psychiatric hospital admissions have been in the winter. Her suicide attempts have also been in this season. SAD affects the body's natural balance by targeting the circadian rhythms when there are seasonal changes. I dread autumn and winter, though prior to Karla's SAD diagnosis I would look forward to autumn. It feels so fresh and the colours of the leaves on the trees are beautiful.

Sunshine is an excellent cure, that's why the holiday to Spain from the Not Forgotten Association was so vital for her. It was lovely to see her smile and laugh again. The company of others helped enormously as well.

We get little sunshine from September here in Scotland, though it is glorious when we get it. However, we have some coping mechanisms in place to help her.

Scattered around the house are special SAD light therapy lamps that mimic sunshine as well as brightening up the rooms. We have them in the lounge, kitchen and at her desk. They are perfect for doing my tapestries, as they are the brightest lights in the house. They are ideal for reading the small print on labels and for doing my crosswords. Karla even has one that mimics sunset and dawn so that her circadian rhythms can get into a regular pattern. They are quite expensive though, as are their replacement bulbs. She also has one that sits on her head, like a baseball cap, and projects the light around her forehead. They are worth every penny to keep Karla from harming herself.

Vitamin D is normally gained through sunshine and though it can be found in some foods, the dosage needed to combat SAD is much higher. Karla takes a daily supplement which we have on our regular order from ASDA. Getting outside all year round helps. I get my supply topped up by going into the garden to feed the birds and then taking Lynne out for a gentle stroll.

Karla has a wide circle of friends and needs encouraging to go along to her crafting classes and meeting them at cafes and in their homes. Friendships are great therapy. Though low concentration is a symptom of SAD, it is so vital to encourage her to see her chums. There is a pattern prior to her admissions to the hospital where she stops seeing her pals, replying to texts, joining in WhatsApp conversations, or going silent on Facebook. As a coping mechanism, I boot her out of the door and get her to see them. It then gives me and Lynne some alone time!

If you think your mood and concentration dips from September and you are feeling lethargic or uninterested in your usual activities and hobbies, please consider getting the special lamps and taking Vitamin D. You may wish to consult your GP first. And then keep up your visits to your pals. Don't be a hermit like me. I know it isn't healthy, but I love my own and Lynne's company above all others. She's my best friend.

CHAPTER 30:

PANIC ATTACKS AND MY FAVOURITE COPING MECHANISMS

My first panic attack was scary. It happened soon after developing PTSD and is tied in with my anxiety. The room spins around; I have double vision and see rapid, darting lights. I feel sick from the dizziness and know I am going to collapse. I break out into a cold, clammy sweat. There is an overwhelming need to run, to flee from the stimuli. As a double-whammy, I also get flashbacks. I hate those helicopters that fly above my Aberdeenshire home.

I still get panic attacks. Usually, when I let my anxiety over Angus, Abigail, Karla, and my PTSD get out of control. But I've learnt to control this monster. I shut down. It may look rude and odd to others. I find a seat or lie down. I breathe. I concentrate on each breath, nice and slowly. I inhale through my nose for four seconds, then exhale through my mouth for six seconds to rid myself of any tension. I breathe deeply. This is a great technique for all the symptoms that I've described in the previous chapters. This is the chapter where I reveal my favourite coping mechanisms because you'll need them if, like me, you have depression, anxiety, PTSD, and panic attacks. It's all about the breathing, trying to relax, dropping those tense shoulders, allowing your arms, hands, and legs to go limp and floppy.

Forget everything else and just breathe. Keep this pattern of four to six going until you feel your pulse slow and panic recede. Then sit up slowly and stand in your own good time. Then you are good to go.

Anything that will unknot the tension in your neck and shoulders will help reduce your anxiety and, with it, your panic attacks. Have a massage from a qualified therapist as often as possible. Especially if the professional also uses aromatherapy oils, which helps reduce stress. Lavender is fantastically relaxing. I put it in my bath and mix it with my hand cream. Its aroma is very grounding. Get an egg cup, put a few drops of baby oil in, and then add some lavender. This helps to diffuse the healing stuff in the aromatherapy oils. Run this mixture under your bath tap and it gives you the most relaxing bath. Lie back and find your inner peace. It's also great for your skin.

Use the five senses technique where you allow your mind to concentrate on what is around you. It grounds you and brings you back to reality. It is great for coping with flashbacks. For example, if you have food or drink by you, then you could taste it, sniff it, feel the food, cup, or plate, listen to what is going on around you and zone into a relaxing sound, like bird chatter or water. Or create your own relaxing sound like music. That's why I always wear my noise-cancelling headphones. I have certain songs I can access within seconds.

Then see one object, really look at it and explore it. Build up to five other objects. Do the same for your other senses. Make sure you've gone through all five senses of seeing, hearing, touching, tasting, and smelling, building up from one to five. This should ground you, bring you back to reality, and stop your panic attack. Don't worry if you can't do all five senses. Four will work just as well.

As another example, you could be in a supermarket and get a panic attack in the vegetable aisle because of the blaring music, overhead fans, or the crowds of shoppers. Use a technique taught to me by a counsellor. She got me to recall the smell I associated with my dear

Nana. I remembered her Lux soap smell and though I couldn't find bars of this soap in shops; I found some on eBay. I bought a box load. Using it in my daily bath is reassuring. The counsellor advised me to wet a cotton handkerchief and then rub the soap into it and allow it to dry. I keep this in my pocket and during a panic attack I simply reach into my pocket and give the Lux aroma a discrete sniff, feel along it, hear my breath, and look along the cotton. To other shoppers and staff, it'll look like I am blowing my nose or stifling a sneeze. Besides, who cares what others think? I don't! Think about what smell would reassure you and how you can carry it around with you.

During the above, you could visualise a favourite place, or an imaginary spot, like near a stream, or a favourite walk. Think about the surroundings. Remember the bay in Cyprus my psychologist took me to whenever EMDR overwhelmed me? I go there every day, sometimes several times a day. I hear the gentle lap of the water. I can taste and smell the salty sea; I look at the beach, the fine-grained sand running through my hand as I pick up a handful, and then I see the deep blue waters, surrounded by rocks. I take the visualisation one step further and imagine myself on a sun lounger, laid back, enjoying the sun, as Bessie and Bouncer frolic in the sea whilst Lynne is laid by me. I reach out and stroke her.

Imagine whatever works for you and keeps you calm. Divert your mind. You deserve to be taken to a lovely place.

Try adding positive affirmations as you breathe in and out. Imagine yourself saying something like, 'I will sleep well' or 'I am calm.' Whatever works for you. Another is 'I am safe.' You could say these aloud or in your head.

Lynne is so attuned to me when I get anxious or have a panic attack. I think I exude a distinct odour and she cleverly smells the change in my body's chemicals. Or perhaps it's my body language or tenseness. She comes straight to me, nudges my hand, or jumps onto my shoulders, places a paw on either side and presses her nose to mine, or snuggles into my neck. She helps me with the five senses of seeing her being protective to my needs, hearing her soft breathing, sniffing that great dog smell, and having skin to fur contact. Mind you, it looks odd when I taste her and get a mouth full of hair! Gawds!

The only homework I want you to do today is to think about your panic symptoms and learn how to tame them by doing the relaxation and coping techniques I've described. I have more of them to tell you, but first, more symptoms of grief and PTSD.

CHAPTER 31:

FEELING OF DREAD

I hate this one with great venom. Dread creeps up on me like an assassin with a knife. It starts in my groin area as a dull, heavy ache. I feel like something bad is going to happen, but I don't know what. It then travels to my gut and may be a contributing factor to my stomach problems. I think it stems from being told the worst thing has happened, the death of my son.

Yet, what else could be as bad as that? The death of Lynne, Abigail, or Karla. This can have me in knots. I'll start wringing my hands, as if washing the blood of the aircrew off me. Then it's knee and thigh stroking – my imaginary cleaning of my blood caked trousers. The wiggling of my toes, squelching in blood that has seeped through my lightweight tropical canvas boots and socks.

I dread knocks on the door and telephone calls. We experienced both, as the police couldn't rouse us from our drug-addled sleep. We were both on, and still are, high levels of prescribed sedation. I can no longer go to bed before 1am. That's the time when our world stopped.

It can take days to shake off this awful feeling. My best cure has been Lynne. Whenever I feel these symptoms creeping up, she places a gentle muzzle on my knee. My hand wringing and imaginary cleaning ceases and I pet and make a fuss over her. She loves strokes and cuddles as much as I do. She is susceptible to an ear scratch. We are perfectly suited. She calms me down and distracts me. Life was awful before she came to her forever home. I don't know how I survived after Angus's death. Now the assassin doesn't get anywhere near me – Lynne chases him away. His knife gets nowhere near my body and no harm falls upon me when I have my faithful watcher looking after me.

Recognise these symptoms in yourself. They are common after losing a child to suicide and can also affect those living with PTSD. Find your own coping strategies and read on. If you've flicked to this chapter, please take time to read the previous one, where I revealed my other best coping strategies. There's more to follow, but first, just one last symptom in the complexity of having military PTSD and paternal grief. It's so important to recognise our symptoms because then we can cope better with them, and I hope I'm teaching you to lead a better life by sharing my experiences and how I overcame them.

CHAPTER 32:

PARANOIA

Some people may hear nearby laughter and imagine the gathered group are talking about them. This is nothing compared to the paranoia I've developed since having military PTSD. In the early days, before treatment and gaining a deeper understanding of my condition, I was hyper-alert and vigilant, so much so that I was paranoid about the least little thing. If someone walked past the house, idly admiring our elephant window décor on the front door, I would think that they were casing out the joint, like in a ham Hollywood film. I'd be on edge, expecting a knock on the door, or overnight intruders. I would sleep lightly, prepared to reach out to the nearby baseball bat. Paranoia isn't rational.

I would be constantly scanning the supermarket aisles and turning around in the queues. On the few occasions when we were at a cafe or restaurant, I would check the entrance for new arrivals, and then scrutinise the other customers at the tables. If someone was looking at me, or in my direction, probably innocently looking out of the nearby window, I'd be imagining all sorts. I'd then have to leave.

Being arrested by the police didn't help me. Nor did their 1am arrival to bring us the news every parent dreads. I came to despise the knock on the door or doorbell. Even if it was someone as innocent as a window cleaner touting for new business, or the postie with a parcel.

With the paranoia comes anxiety, that chest crushing feeling and it brings my old friend dread. It's a vicious cycle that needs breaking.

The high level of drugs I'm now taking helps keep my paranoia at bay, as does Lynne. I'm too busy keeping her from being naughty to worry about anything or anyone else. She's a great distraction. She isn't really naughty, she's lovely and responds well to her training.

Though I slip occasionally. The most recent was a man who followed me around a supermarket cafe, firing questions about my service life and PTSD. Getting fed up with his insensitivity, I told him, in detail, about some things I've had to do. His pale face was a picture to see, and it stopped him dead in his tracks and he left me alone to refill my coffee mug and get cutlery. Then I had a cuddle with Lynne and calmed down and together, we booted paranoia out of the door. Then we tucked into our Big Scottish Breakfast – don't tell my GP, or the nurse who takes my blood for cholesterol levels. Lynne's favourite is the Lorne Sausage, but don't tell Bravehound!

Recognise the signs in yourself and talk them over with your health care professional and family and then try some of the breathing or distraction methods I've spoken about in previous chapters and those to come.

CHAPTER 33:

SWEATING AND GOING THERMONUCLEAR

My old friend, PTSD, causes me to break out into hot and cold sweats throughout the day and night. It always happens during flashbacks and nightmares. It occurs when I am in queues, when my triggers blast off, and when my exit is blocked. People around me are shivering, in the Scottish weather, but I am going to what I call Thermonuclear level. Now I know how menopausal ladies feel during a hot flush. I wish I'd listened to more Woman's Hour on Radio 4. I may have learned new coping strategies.

I remember when I was a student nurse on a medical ward at the Queen Elizabeth Military Hospital in Woolwich. During the handover, where the nurse going off shift reports vital information about patients to the new shift, a ward Sister would spring off her chair, thrust open the window, and stick her head out for a few minutes. Bits of paper would fly off the desk and we mortals, in our white tunics or grey dresses, would shiver from the winter frosts and winds assaulting the office. By the way, I wasn't in a grey dress! I think Sister may have been menopausal.

I also go to Thermonuclear level in uncomfortable situations, like when folk question me about my PTSD. You won't believe how insensitive and nosey some folks are. And persistent. It's worse now that I have Lynne. People think they can come up and stroke her. One lady, a total stranger, squatted down and embraced me for a minute. I try to control my symptoms, especially my temper. I've also had folk interrupt my training, out in the open, in shops and even at the boot of my car, wanting to know what I'm doing and how they can train their own dog. I always recommend Denise at Awesome Paws to them. Then give them Lynne's social media pages and Bravehound web address and ask them to leave a donation - that usually gets rid of them.

If this happens to you too, here's how I overcome it. I wear layers during the winter so I can strip off. My last layer is always the thinnest of t-shirts. I wear lightweight trousers and socks wherever possible. As an example, I was assessed for an army disability pension recently. There were a lot of questions and the door to the claustrophobic room was shut. As each question was fired at me, I became Thermonuclear and stripped off a layer each time I answered them, until I was down to my trusty old, wafer-thin, Dalek t-shirt. The doctor and Karla were wearing jumpers and gilets.

If you see me lifting my arms like I'm doing a bird impression, that's me just airing my armpits, trying to get cool. I also carry a handkerchief, so I can discreetly wipe my forehead and neck.

I sleep in the coldest bedroom; the radiator is rarely on. The window air vents are open, and I use a 1 tog duvet. I take this to hotels when I am down at Bravehound HQ and am staying overnight. It even came to Jersey with us when we had the lovely Holidays for Heroes Jersey break. Karla has her half with a thicker duvet of a higher tog rating, or an extra blanket. Though we try to book twin beds if the hotel or B&B doesn't have a King-sized bed so that my nightmare thrashing doesn't accidentally hit Karla.

Lynne radiates a lot of body heat too and prefers my side of the bed as we spoon and cuddle. Occasionally, she lets me embrace Karla!

Have a name for when this happens to you. Explain it to your friends and family and describe how it makes you feel so they can support you in cooling and calming down.

CHAPTER 34:

LOW CONCENTRATION

I love reading, anything from novels, magazines and even comics like 2000AD and Judge Dredd. Yet, after losing Angus, it took me more than two years before I picked anything up to read. This was down to my depression, but also because of a low concentration level. There was also a lot of thinking I didn't deserve pleasure while my son lay in his cold grave. Learning to live through grief and coping with PTSD had sapped my energy. I would read a page of a book but would have to re-read it several times, as I couldn't retain what I'd read.

I turned to passive things to fill my day and evening. This was predominantly television. I became a couch potato. My weight ballooned and so did my apathy. The postie diligently delivered my subscription magazines and comics and I duly picked them up from the porch and placed them on a growing and groaning pile in my study.

I didn't even keep in my mind what I'd watched on TV and would often record repeats and watch them with Karla and she'd point out we'd seen it before. I had no recollection. I was mentally ill for months until I was guided onto the correct pathway by my counsellor and GP.

I have no recollection of people and conversations and I felt shame when I met Lee again at Bravehound and had to ask who he was when Lynne remembered him and went running across and placed her paws on his shoulder for a cuddle. Lee had assessed me the previous December and had taught Lynne as a puppy to cuddle on command. I owe a lot to Lee and his diligent training. Cuddle is the most useful of her commands and keeps me from going to Thermonuclear level and eases my flashbacks, nightmares, and anxiety.

It was the peaceful John Paul's Retreat that re-ignited my love for crosswords and the Not Forgotten Association Spanish holiday at the delightful villa that brought colour back into my life and my love for Doctor Who returned. Reading my magazines at the poolside was so relaxing and the Spanish sunshine brought the photos on the pages to life.

Take each day as it comes. Don't put pressure on yourself, or allow others to pressurise you. One day, your concentration will improve, and you'll find a zest for those activities and hobbies you previously loved prior to your loss or diagnosis.

CHAPTER 35:

WHAT IF...

The What If questions will eat you up and destroy you. When there is a sudden death, like in a car accident or suicide, there are so many unanswered questions. There has been no chance to say, 'I love you,' and to hear it back. I'd say it is more so with a suicide because not all people who take their own lives will leave a final note or letter. In our case, the police denied there were any letters. We gained entry to Angus's flat ten days later, after the police had completed their investigations and had removed the gigantic bolt and padlock from his door. There we found a torn-up suicide letter to his friends. Thank heavens for the apparent incompetence of the police. Otherwise, Karla, Abigail and I would have been imagining all sorts. As it was, he explained in his letter to his friends what happened to him and why he'd taken his life. He also told them not to tell us. He was protecting us from his pain. But knowing why he'd taken his life didn't bring us any succour. It brought us much anguish knowing what he'd kept to himself.

I don't think I'll ever be free of the What Ifs, but I am now much more rational and in a better place. I can mentally bat them away and concentrate on all the fun and good times Angus brought to Karla, Abigail, and myself. It has taken much therapy and several years to get to this stage.

My What Ifs centred around questioning if I'd been a better father, would Angus have opened up to me and then I could have got him the psychological support and treatment he needed to cope in the aftermath of the monstrous crime he fell victim to. Each day, I would explore mentally how I could have been a better dad. I questioned my style of parenting and whether I was a good husband and if I was being a supportive father to Abigail. Years later, I had my answer. It was staring me in the face all along. Abigail has blossomed into a caring young woman who is well-educated and is on a career to be a counsellor or psychotherapist. She lives near us, currently in Angus's flat, and we see her often and she talks openly to us. Karla and I brought up two lovely children. She has met a pleasant man, and it is so wonderful to see her in love and being loved.

It was a brave decision for her to take ownership of the flat, the place where Angus took his life. I've never been back, but she has decorated, had a new kitchen installed and made it her own. She wanted to live there, to be closer to him. She keeps his clothes in their wardrobe. He left few possessions. He'd given away most of his things, or sold them, wanting to tie up any loose ends.

Another What If that really ate me up was learning, after Angus's suicide, that he'd confided to some of his friends that he was going to do it. None of them took him to his GP or Casualty for immediate help and to keep him safe. No one told us so that we could envelop Angus in a cocoon and keep him safe until his mind was more balanced. I had to stay away from his friends because I was so angry with them. I didn't enter McDonald's for about two years. I was too frightened that I may erupt and that my anger would damage someone.

My rational mind kicked in about two years later and I knew his work friends were of his age, or younger. They would have had no medical training, nor mental health first aid training. They would not have known how to talk to Angus, to keep him safe and get him to the help he deserved. It wasn't their fault.

I later learned that his branch of McDonald's brought someone in to teach each crew member how to respond to someone with suicidal intent and how to keep them safe and get them help. I believe this may happen nationwide in all their branches – but it's too late for our dear Angus.

There have also been many What Ifs about the dead people who haunt my nightmares and flashbacks. What If I'd got to them sooner? What If we'd kept up the cardiac compressions during the CPR cycles? What If we'd done one more cycle. What If we could have? Try not to go there. It took me a long time to rationalise that the teams and I did all we could for each patient.

Do yourself a big favour, don't beat yourself up. It wasn't your fault. You know deep down you would have got your loved one the help they needed and would have kept them safe.

We had to do this with Abigail when she broke down a year after Angus's death. She texted she didn't want to live anymore. We brought her home and watched over her until the emergency psychiatric team, our family doctor, and PTSD Resolution expertly kept her safe and treated her. A year later she had another breakdown at work, and her managers and colleagues stepped in and kept her safe, for which they have my eternal thanks.

If you have many What Ifs from your military experience, try to rationalise that you and your comrades did all you could. You will have remembered your training, followed, or given the correct orders in difficult circumstances and adhered to standard operating procedures.

My top tip is to get the family or military photo albums out and remember the good times. Honour the memory of your loved one or friend by learning to live the best life you can.

CHAPTER 36:

ANSWERS

One item Angus did not sell, or giveaway, was a large cashbox. It was locked. It rattled when I shook it. There was something in it. It had a combination lock, so I stayed up and tried every combination until it finally opened to reveal – nothing. The rattle was coming from the coin tray. My heart sank.

I had hoped it contained some answers or perhaps a letter to his mum, sister, or me. Sometimes there are no answers. I hate to say this phrase, but sometimes they take their secrets to their graves. I'm reminded of Angus's torn-up letter to his friends, and I will say an addendum to that awful phrase. Sometimes they try.

There may be no answers to your questions. This will also eat you up if you let it. There will come a time where you will enter one specific stage of grieving. I learned about it early in my student nurse training – acceptance. It'll bring you peace of mind.

You've probably already worked through the other stages of shock, denial, bargaining and anger. There is no order to having them and not everyone goes through each stage. Most people flit between them and go back to others. These were first described by Dr Elisabeth Kübler-Ross in 1969. Her book, On Death and Dying, was a useful text to read as a junior student nurse. Years later, as a grieving father, I flitted in and out of each stage, some I returned to, but eventually I accepted. I can look back on my grief route and can see how ill I became, how angry I was, and how shocked I was upon hearing the news from the police.

Years later, after finishing the first draft of this book, I recognised I was entering another period of depression and my anxiety was threatening to get out of control. I mentally took a step back and asked myself why. I worked out that these symptoms were related to my headphones losing their effectiveness. I couldn't afford another pair, so I reached out to Help for Heroes. I was assigned a diligent case worker called Jock. He and my initial assessor, Karen, encouraged me to enrol into their free courses. These were done online, for an hour or two a week. I could cope with that and my caring responsibilities. On one module, What is Recovery, I learned that Dr Elisabeth Kübler-Ross also theorised a change curve. I recognised her stages of shock and denial, but saw that she had added four more. These were depression, experiment, decision, and integration. The symptoms of depression were given as low mood and lacking energy – I ticked that box. Then the curve rose to three levels. The first was experiment, where the person initially engages with the new decision. I was part way there by acknowledging that I have PTSD. Writing this book has helped me see that and kicked away my denial. No matter how much I don't like it, I have military PTSD and a chunk of that is seeing Angus in the mortuary. I was heartened to see I could go higher on the curve towards decision. The Help for Heroes slide and booklet stated this as learning how to work in the new situation and feeling more positive. I was half in that category. I was learning to live without Angus and with PTSD, but I certainly wasn't feeling positive about it. I don't think I ever will. The final stage was integration where the changes are implemented and, through personal growth, the individual is renewed. I know I've become the new me, however reluctantly. Dr Elisabeth Kübler-Ross' model allows the individual to reach certain stages, to go back, or not to reach certain points, throughout their lives. But still no answers.

But it didn't stop me looking for answers from any source. The Procurator Fiscal office here in Scotland not only deals in criminal acts but also is in overall charge of death by suicide investigations. As part of their enquiries, they contacted me, and a patient man guided me through the process and asked if I had questions. I had loads, and he took the time to answer them all. Then he surprised me by asking if I would like a copy of Angus's post-mortem results. I was a little taken aback but said yes. These were e-mailed to me, and I didn't find any answers there either, other than discovering that Angus was fit and well, had no drugs in his blood and a small amount of alcohol, barely enough to measure one unit.

Do look for answers, but one day you should try to accept, however reluctantly, that there may be no answers. Your peace of mind is a valuable healing gift that only yourself can give.

CHAPTER 37:

IMPOSTER SYNDROME

Imposter Syndrome is where you think you don't deserve your success or doubt your ability in a role, despite having been trained or having skills. I've suffered from this since the day I qualified as a Staff Nurse. I'd passed all the exams to become a Registered General Nurse after three years of training, but I can still recall the first day I was placed in charge of a medical ward at the QEMH. I was terrified! There were no Ward Sisters to advise me, nor other RGNs. I had responsibility for about 32 patients and around 5 to 10 staff. My colleagues comprised Enrolled Nurses, Student Nurses, and Health Care Assistants (though in my era of being qualified, they were called Ward Stewardesses and were primarily responsible for the catering welfare of patients, cleaning, stores, etc. They also performed a good deal of health-related tasks such as taking temperatures and pulses and I was pleased to see their training and responsibilities extend to HCA level a few years later). The patients varied from tests for ulcerative colitis, living with Parkinson's disease, being diagnosed with cancer or HIV and AIDS, through to diagnosis and treatment of multiple sclerosis and diabetes. It was quite a responsibility ensuring all their needs were met, doing my first solo drugs round and Matron's report.

I questioned whether I deserved to be there, whether I had earned the increase in pay and responsibility, and whether I was up to the job. Then the excellent training I underwent from the fantastic tutors kicked in and I got over myself and knuckled down to some hard work.

It was the same when I was promoted to the dizzy heights of Lance Corporal. Was I a junior leader? Did I have the talent, skills, and charisma to be in charge? Yes, I was, and I'd passed the army course in junior leadership, where I returned to Keogh Barracks again. Only this time I had been re-badged to the Queen Alexandra's Royal Army Nursing Corps, commonly known as the QAs. Or the Grey Mafia! This nickname was because of the grey beret and grey ward dresses worn. I never got a dress when us males joined the female dominated QA world. I didn't have the legs for it! The beret stood out like a sore thumb in a sea of black berets with maroon Royal Army Medical Corps cap badge backing. During the junior leadership course, the fierce RAMC drill sergeant and his corporals loved sending me to the jail for being a QA. There I met some more delightful RAMC corporals who enjoyed exercising me some more. I got fitter but didn't learn a great deal of leadership skills from them. Though I did in the classroom work and these skills were put to good use in the service hospitals and later in the nursing homes I worked in when I left the army.

Incidentally, I became a QA on the First of April 1992. I was serving in the military hospital at Airport Camp, Belize. There were three of us RAMC male nurses working at the hospital, and we thought it was an elaborate April Fool's Day joke. We were lined up for an inspection and belt and beret handover by the Commanding Officer. She explained there were no grey berets nor the scarlet and grey buckle belts. Instead, we were each handed a photocopy of the QA cap badge and told to continue wearing our RAMC beret, cap badge, and belts. Yeah, it was a prank, we all thought. Work continued and when I was posted back to the Cambridge Military Hospital, in Aldershot, I not only learned that I'd been promoted, but the kindly Matron advised me to get to the clothing store because I was inappropriately dressed in the wrong beret and belt. And so, I joined the Grey Mafia. I wish the kindly Matron had overseen the Regimental Association when SSAFA contacted them for help. Perhaps she would have aided me.

A bigger imposter syndrome I felt, and sometimes still do, is over whether I deserved to be assisted by the military charities. It wasn't helped when week after week my diligent SSAFA case worker got knock back after knock back from the major military charities. It didn't help when Combat Stress discharged me over the phone and failed to provide the local support they had promised me.

When I went to Holidays for Heroes Jersey, I felt an imposter. The others had taken part in major campaigns and wars. Some bore the physical scars and the mental ones. That phrase, 'I was just a nurse,' kept popping into my head. Yet the other veterans and their families accepted Karla and me and we enjoyed their company. I rarely spoke about my service career and told few that I see dead people in flashbacks and in nightmares. I was worried they would think me barmy.

I still had it when Karla was invited to the Buckingham Palace tea party and the Spanish holiday by the Not Forgotten Association. Yet, she qualified because of her disability. Again, I spoke rarely of my service career. I wasn't ashamed of my service record. It was exemplary when described in my annual reports. I went to where I was posted and nursed and soldiered to the best of my ability.

There was one major imposter syndrome hurdle I had to overcome, and that was whether I should take an assistance dog from Bravehound, when another, more deserving veteran should have it. I'm glad I did. I love my Lynne. I can't imagine life without her. But that old denial struck and tussled with imposter syndrome and mixed my emotions and thoughts. Despite so many health care professionals diagnosing my PTSD, I still questioned if I should have a PTSD assistance dog. I'm glad I won the wrestle. Lynne is the best thing that's happened to me in years.

I even had it over Angus's death and questioned if I was a good enough father to feel this amount of grief and pain. It had me curled up in a ball and wanting to die; I thought I had imposter syndrome. The human mind is a fragile and complex organ. Mine was frazzled.

None of this helped my mental health, and it declined further. I really was ill and in the next chapter I'll talk about one other symptom many of us with PTSD wrestle with.

Acknowledge imposter syndrome in yourself and get rational. You may find it beneficial to write five things that you excelled at in your military career. You've served your country, are not an imposter, and deserve the care of the military charities. That is why they were set up. They want to help veterans like us get back on our feet and stay there. Don't be shy about seeking help.

If you are a grieving relative or friend, acknowledge these feelings and write about the happy times and the occasions you really supported and encouraged those you have lost. Honour those you have loved in your happy memories. Let's turn those negative thoughts into positive ones.

CHAPTER 38:

SURVIVOR'S GUILT

Going hand in hand with imposter's syndrome is survivor's guilt. I didn't get this with the number of deaths I have been involved with in my caring capacity as a nurse and medic. I rarely knew many of the accident deaths, though I got to know many of the patients and their loved ones who I'd nursed prior to their deaths. These gave me no survivor's guilt. Many deaths were expected, others were sudden. In all cases, I nursed them to the best of my ability. There was no fault on my part.

I've always admired the way soldiers in regiments form close friendships and I have often seen the way they pull together when one of them is injured or suffers from a life-changing disease. At its extreme, after the death of the Tornado crew, the surviving Squadron would have held the traditional auction of their gear and some of their personal kit. This is primarily to raise funds for the surviving family and helps to sanitise the items handed over to the family so they see nothing disturbing. I don't know if the Army or Royal Navy do this too.

Going into battle cements comradeship like no other. I think that is why some will develop survivor's guilt. The big, "Why me?" doubt. Often it has no rationality. It was the enemy who pulled the fatal trigger or planted the improvised explosive device. It wasn't the survivor's fault, yet many in the Armed Forces have survivor's guilt. More so, for those who swapped a duty, for example, in which that person then lost their life. I can only imagine the ruminations that go on in survivor's minds. It must be equally awful to have watched mates die in such appalling ways.

My survivor's guilt comes from Angus. Mainly, why am I, at fifty-three, having had a full life, still alive, when my dear son died at twenty-two? I'd swap places with him in a heartbeat. But sadly, life doesn't work that way. I've seen too many men in their twenties die from heart attacks, cancer, heatstroke during runs in Belize and Cyprus, vehicle crashes, and from training exercises that went wrong. I've seen first-hand just how cruel life can be. I guess it's the same for other parents whose children die young. It's the cruellest of life's curveballs.

For this reason, I found it hard to pick up a book and enjoy reading once more because I thought I didn't deserve to be happy again, not after losing Angus in such a tragic way. It's the same for other hobbies like listening to a Doctor Who Big Finish drama or a simple walk down to the harbour on a beautiful day. I shunned going out for meals. Anything that I derived pleasure from, I detested. It just seemed plain wrong to be happy and find pleasure again. This passed, given time, though I slip back into it now and again.

Therapy helped too. In fact, it played the biggest part in resolving this. My dark and disturbing thoughts were challenged by three counsellors, a psychologist, and my GP. I was taught the importance of rewarding myself with pleasurable things again and taking time out for myself. I bought books and picked up magazines and newspapers. I watched my Doctor Who DVDs and streamed Picard on Amazon Prime. I even watched the old comedies on ITV3, my favourite being On the Buses and, ironically, That's my Boy.

It's hard to do, but given time you can retrain your brain to move away from survivor's guilt and to see, rationally, that it wasn't your fault. You loved and should cherish the memories of your family member or friend. I don't like the phrase "Time is a great healer" but believe, instead, that time allows you to receive professional guidance and support to look back at events, understand them and then build a new life for yourself.

CHAPTER 39:

BEING HYPER

I feel many jumbled thoughts rushing through my brain; I get restless, feel the need to run, though my damaged legs say otherwise. I talk fast and furious and jump between conversations. I also get easily side-tracked, oh, look, there's a blue tit at the feeder. Watch my fidgety, tapping hands or pumping legs. See me get up and down from my seat. Observe me roam from room to room. All at ninety miles an hour. I've never felt hyperactivity like it. This is PTSD without medical treatment and the correct dosage of the right medication.

Things are much calmer now. I'm more at peace with myself. Lynne calms me down. She's a very soothing presence. Her fur is so silky and I love to stroke her. She cherishes the attention. It's a win-win.

I can recognise these signs in my fellow veterans with PTSD and I bet they recognise them in me. I've seen the agitation in them before they board a plane – they hate air travel as much as I do. They pace around the airport. Being confined in a tin box hurtling through the air isn't our idea of fun.

I witness them talking ten to the dozen about absolute gobbledegook.

I've seen another immediately strip off and jump into a swimming pool when it was inappropriate.

Another taps out rhythms on tables, armrests, any surface.

We all feel the need to rush, run, and escape these feelings.

I got little hyper-activity with the death of Angus. It was the opposite. There was depression. I was angry, but I didn't have a decent outlet for it. I tried fast walks, but my painful legs screamed in protest. Then apathy struck, and I took to my bed, or slumped in my armchair.

My hyperactivity is made worse by caffeinated drinks, especially coffee. Sugar affects it too. I tried to give up both, otherwise it affects my sleep, particularly the coffee. It could be my age, or general low activity because of my aching limbs, but it takes a good twelve hours for the coffee-induced anxiety and hyperactivity to rid itself, even though I take high doses of sedatives.

Try to give up these foods and drinks and see if it helps lower your arousal levels. I've switched to sugar free squashes and decaffeinated coffee and tea and limit these. Water is much better for me, and you.

Take your medicines! Find a compassionate GP who empathises with PTSD and visit him or her regularly.

CHAPTER 40:

SHEDDING EXCESS BAGGAGE

I'm now going to drill down to more specific coping mechanisms for grief and PTSD. Some may not affect you, and I hope this chapter doesn't. It may be the most painful one to do. I'd advise you to talk this through with a good friend, close relative, or health care professional.

I've spoken earlier in this book about my mother and father's reaction to the death of Angus. In case you skipped those chapters, I'll do a brief recap. Several hours after we learned of Angus's suicide, we went to my parent's house as early as we could. This was before we could view Angus's body at the police mortuary at the designated time allotted to us. It was early morning. We sat my parents down and broke the news as calmly as we could. Dad's first response was to ask a strange question. He wanted to know if two specific relatives could come to the funeral. I said no. One had replicated my business model, twice, and I'd lost a great deal of money through my naïve trust. Another had been accused of child sexual abuse by another relative. I wanted neither of them at my son's funeral. I'd had nothing to do with both relatives for years. Nor had Angus.

Dad was enraged. I put this down to the shock of learning about the death of his only grandson. This was the last time he spoke to me. I received a text later that day from him. It was not nice. Neither of my parents came to my house to pay their respects or to support Abigail,

Karla, and me.

On the day of the funeral, dad did not speak to me. Not one word. Nor did I feel his supportive hand on my shoulder or wrapped around me. I desperately needed someone to unburden some of my pain. I needed someone to talk to. They were the only relatives not to take one of my prized white fantail doves and release them from their box at the graveside.

My parents have never asked why Angus took his life. I needed someone to share this emotional burden with. A year later, the psychologist helped me see they are emotionally bereft and have never been there for me. I made the painful decision to shed this excess baggage from my mind and ceased trying. It was as if a tremendous burden was lifted from my shoulders and helped me heal a little better.

I've since met someone who thought they were being supported by a friend who was a solicitor and was guiding this person through the painful and complicated legal circumstances of the suicide of their child. Their friendship continued and then the solicitor friend sent an enormous bill for all work carried out. It gave the person an immense shock and wake-up call. Sadly, there are people who will take advantage of you during your grief or illness. Keep your wits about you.

If you find yourself in the situation where someone is causing you a great deal of emotional pain, then perhaps you too need to question their value in your life and maybe move on from them. But keep those who love and support you close to your chest, hug, embrace, love and cherish them. They are priceless and you need good buddies in your fight against grief and PTSD.

CHAPTER 41:

LEARNING TO SAY NO

This is a skill I have had to develop. I'm a people-pleaser. I guess it comes from my nurturing and caring nursing side. The power of you saying yes is only as strong as when you say no. And sometimes, for your own health and mental wellbeing, you will need to say no.

I featured in a local newspaper a few years ago. They ran a story about my book, Buried in Grief, and the angle the reporter published is that I wrote it to help me deal with my son's death. Unfortunately, it came across as sounding as a self-help book for other parents. Anyone who has read that novel will know it is anything but! I know, right! That ending! What was I thinking? But I so love me a bit of horror writing, it unleashes my dark side. It's quite therapeutic in its own way. But not for some. As a result, several lovely folks asked me to speak to their support groups. I hope it helped them.

I hate public speaking and was a bundle of nerves beforehand, even though my clever Lynne was by my side. Let's just say I needed an ample supply of toilet paper, and we'll leave it there!

I met some strong people who were learning to live with a range of similar conditions to me, like anxiety, grief, and PTSD. I hope it helped them to see that life can go on after a major bereavement and developing a debilitating condition.

I was asked by one group to get more involved. This would have resulted in me writing out letters, keeping accounts, and other secretarial work. At the same time, the support group Karla and I attended for survivors of suicide was about to fold. It needed a new co-ordinator. This would have meant the new person doing the same type and level of secretarial work, but also receiving phone calls and meeting the newly bereaved prior to the support group meetings.

I gave each role careful consideration, then weighed up my own mental health needs, the running of our household, caring for Karla, and my work in trying to write more novels and succeeding in the self-publishing world. I had to say no – I was taking on too much, and I knew I wouldn't have coped. It wouldn't have been fair to either organisation, or to the people I'd have to have met. I could barely cope looking after myself and Karla without the added burden of other's grief. Besides, I didn't have access to a car, and it would have involved two bus trips and several hours of journeys and waiting each time.

Looking back, it was the right decision. Several years later, I reflect and think I could take on either of those roles now.

I learnt the power of saying no. Since then, I'm learning to put my own needs first and have said no to other people without the guilt that used to have me tied up in knots. It's a skill that takes time to master and I weigh this up with saying lots of yesses to balance and when I say aye, I give my full attention and commitment.

Make your own judgements, don't let others pressure you. Consider requests carefully and weigh up if you can commit and are strong enough to carry out what others want you to do. Your time and money are precious. Spend them wisely. There is nothing wrong in saying no, so you can have more leisure time or are freer to do more work that pays you.

CHAPTER 42:

PTSD RESOLUTION

Karla has PTSD Resolution on speed-dial in case I have one of my monstrous relapses from my military PTSD. We learnt about them from the other veterans on the Holidays for Heroes Jersey break. Many had benefited from their intervention.

When Abigail broke down, about a year after losing Angus, we tried hard to find her immediate care. We did not want to lose another child to suicide. One in three relatives who have lost someone to suicide takes their own life. This was clear when we went to the Compassionate Friends retreat and heard from other parents who had lost two children to suicide. Losing a child or sibling is crippling. We desperately tried the emergency doctor phone line. It was a weekend, and we were getting tied up in knots with bureaucracy. We couldn't get Abigail to our friendly, caring GP until the surgery opened on the Monday. I tried PTSD Resolution and feel blessed to say they agreed to extend their care to our daughter. We will forever be in their debt.

PTSD Resolution is a military charity who have a nationwide network of trauma therapists who will provide you with counselling in your local area either in person or by phone. This is immediate and free and is for any veteran, reservist, and their families. Their help is for the emergency first aid of any mental health need, including PTSD. You do not need a referral, you or a loved one just needs to provide them with your regimental number, corps or regiment and years of service and other brief details to verify your service. It is a confidential service.

Abigail had about five one-hour sessions with an experienced counsellor, and she helped turn her thought process around by using a treatment called Rewind Therapy, where Abigail was taken to a time prior to the trauma of losing Angus. This enabled her to talk openly about her feelings, without visiting the actual trauma and being exposed to harmful emotions again. It is like reviewing or revisiting events, but in a controlled and dissociative way. You expose yourself to memories without connecting to the emotional and mental impact they create. Just like my psychologist did for me, she trained Abigail in deep breathing techniques and learning to visualise a safe place in her mind. This technique also re-educates the brain to remove the fight-or-flight instincts and replaces them with relaxed thoughts.

They also offer Trauma Awareness Training for Everyone, a one-day online course or bespoke packages, so that you can gain a better understanding of employees and colleagues living with PTSD.

Encourage your loved one to attend a free counselling session when they are in crisis or to call yourself and book an appointment visit

www.ptsdresolution.org

CHAPTER 43:

HYPNOTHERAPY

This chapter will be about doing your own research and learning to take control of your health. I'm going to ask you to take to the internet and read about the benefits of hypnotherapy yourself and to decide if you think it could be a course of treatment you need. I've no experience of it, so can't guide you. What I will say is I considered this to deal with the nocturnal noises we had no control over. I spoke to a few hypnotherapists who told me they could help me ignore the bangs and to not react to them. They also said it would work in the treatment of my military PTSD. I couldn't afford their fees, but perhaps you can. Some were also trained psychologists, psychotherapists, or counsellors and if this is a route you are considering, then perhaps it would be best to look for those. That way, you can have some qualified talking therapy in conjunction.

From my nursing days, I heard from many a patient that a hypnotherapist had helped them to stop smoking or cease over-eating. It had many proven health benefits.

I often wonder if the EMDR treatment I received is hypnosis. Following the waggling finger of the psychologist may have put me in a trance-like state. I'm not qualified to say this, it is simply my opinion.

Your GP surgery should be able to put you in touch with a reputable hypnotist or visit the National Council for Hypnotherapy (NCH) at www.hypnotherapists.org.uk – Perhaps let me know on Facebook, Twitter, or Instagram @CGBUSWELL how you get on, or use the contact form at

www.cgbuswell.com/contact.php

I do, however, have experience of using a professional hypnotist's app on my mobile phone. I use it for when I need to relax and have a spare thirty minutes. I also use it to send me off to sleep. I thoroughly recommend typing in Patrick Browning into the app store. I've purchased several of his sessions, all under a fiver, and I get to keep them for life and can use them on other devices and transfer them when I upgrade my mobile. I particularly recommend his one entitled Anxiety. I also use Relax into Sleep and Relax in Your Garden. I miss the sound of birds chattering when I wear my noise-cancelling headphones and Patrick uses birdsong and the sound of running water, like a gentle stream, to beneficial effect. He has a reassuring and soothing voice, something you should remember if you go to a hypnotherapist. His practice is in Kensington if you live anywhere near there. I don't, but he has given me help and advice via e-mail – there is a handy link on his app.

I use the app often, more so on stressful days or when I can't get a grip of my feelings of dread or anxiety.

Other apps are available, some include bedtime stories for adults read by popular actors. It's all about trial and error and finding the right app for you. Most offer free sessions or a week trial, then there are regular costs, but the price of these should fit most budgets.

CHAPTER 44:

MINDFULNESS

I'm an advocate of mindfulness and believe it can take many forms. It's all a matter of finding what works for you. It is all about the present and getting in touch with the moment and concentrating on your breathing, your thoughts and the sounds and sensations around you. Yoga and Tai-Chi are popular avenues you could explore. I always notice how relaxed Abigail is after her weekly yoga lessons. You can probably find a class to join at your local community, sports centre, or gym.

Remember those five senses and breathing exercises I taught you earlier? That is also mindfulness. It's okay if your mind wanders while doing it, so long as you bring it back to the breathing rhythm.

Visit www.nhs.uk and search for mindfulness to read some helpful fact sheets.

My mindfulness moments are going into the garden with Lynne, cuddling up in the arbour, and watching the wild birds feed from the seeds and fat balls I put out for them. I also like to sit and do my tapestries indoors and outdoors. I love the feel of the wool skeins and the rhythm of pulling the wool through the tapestry backing and forming, over time, patterns and shapes and building to a bigger picture. I'm currently working on a gorgeous tiger with her two cubs.

Writing is also a bit of a mindfulness period for me. I get totally immersed in forming words, sentences, paragraphs, pages, and chapters. My mind is solely on what I am trying to convey to the page. Through my characters, I must describe the five senses on the pages for my readers. Many describe feeling they know my characters so well and feel they are really in the places and events I narrate with words. Perhaps this creates a mindfulness moment for them, too. I hope so.

When I type, I maintain as best a posture as I can and since I wear noise-cancelling headphones, all I hear is the regular sound of my breathing and the rhythmic tapping of my fingers at the keyboard. Many authors use dictation software, but I would miss the feel of the keyboard and the all important cadences.

Abigail gifted me a set of superhero adult colouring in sheets and some felt-tip pens. I love doing them as I get immersed in filling in the colours and building towards a finished picture.

The above three examples are of my mindfulness. It's all about finding what works for you, and taking the time, guilt-free, in doing them. Forget about the household chores. You deserve and need some recharge time. It'll help you be a more rounded person who functions better.

CHAPTER 45:

CHILDHOOD

Whichever therapy you choose, it is probably inevitable that the subject of your childhood will crop up, either by yourself or from your therapist. Our younger years shape us and are our formative years. Even our teenage times mould us into the person we become. I spent my later teenage years in the army, and they moulded me to be resilient, reliable, a team player and self-sufficient. They were happy years. Sadly, prior to then, I had an unhappy childhood.

It was fine where I grew up in East Kilbride; I have most pleasant memories from there. Though I recall being shut out in the backyard with the family dog Lassie and no amount of crying or knocking on the door would allow me entry back in. I do not know how long I was there for, but Lassie came and comforted me. She was a beautiful black Collie and from a young age, I've had a love for dogs. We were inseparable, and I loved taking her for walks when I was a little older. When I was about ten years old, and after we had moved to Garthdee, in Aberdeen, I was heartbroken when she had to be put to sleep and hadn't said goodbye. My parents took her to the vet's and told me she was having a haircut and she never came back. My questions went unanswered, and there was no solace. I can't recall my parents ever cuddling me or telling me they loved me. It may have been a generational thing, but other people of my era tell me their parents loved them.

We moved to Aberdeen when I was six and spent months in my Nana's house until Mum and Dad were given a council house a few streets away. This was an idyllic time. I loved my Nana and her new husband, my new Grandad. I felt loved and wanted by them. I didn't know my father's parents. His dad died when he was young and I think I only met his mother once when I was eight and we had a holiday in Lincolnshire, where my dad is from. She died soon after.

The subject of my childhood was uppermost in my mind during the psychology treatment. My therapist and I explored it together, and she taught me I was a neglected and an abused child. This came as a shock. There was that old denial again, with a good deal of imposter syndrome, too. The subject arose years later when I had a dip and had counselling through Hidden Wounds. I was referred to them by Help for Heroes. I was in denial again and the counsellor gently guided me to realise I was a victim of sexual, emotional, and physical abuse. It was not normal to be beaten, belted and slippered as a child, especially for such a long time. The beatings started after Dad had left Mum to stay in another flat in the next area of Aberdeen. As I've written about earlier, we weren't sure who the woman who answered the door was when my brother and I were sent to bring Dad home. All I know is that Dad and Mum argued a lot thereafter and never seemed happy. There was a lot of shouting and fists and belts flying in my direction. I sought and got refuge at my grandparent's house.

I would go at every opportunity. They listened to me and took an interest in my life, such as how my schooling was going. I tended to their garden and loved watching television with them. It was cosy. We watched Dallas and Coronation Street a lot. They had a lovely Yorkshire Terrier, aptly named Tiny and a budgie called Polly who grandad taught to fly down and peck at his fruit. Tiny was so patient with Polly flying around the lounge.

Their garden was enormous because it was on a corner plot, and I found a friend in the neighbour's son. Shaun was great fun, and we'd play football or kerbie together. There were few cars in the 1970s, so it was safe to throw a ball between the kerbs, hoping it would bounce back. It gave us hours of fun.

They had a large garage and when I hit my teenage years and was more body conscious; I saved up my paper round money and bought some weightlifting equipment and a punch bag. I wanted to bulk up so my father would stop belting me. It didn't work; I was still puny, but it gave me an outlet for my anger. I ran a lot too, especially between jobs. No wonder I was so skinny. I'm not now!

My therapist and I talked about my need to wash, keep myself clean and not be smelling. I told her about my early teenage years. Whenever I walked into the lounge, Dad and Mum seemed to always be watching pornography. This was in the 1980s and a pre-internet age, so it wasn't as readily available for those who like that sort of thing. It was also extreme. It confused my young mind, and I sought refuge at Nana's. She would have been ashamed of her daughter and son-in-law, and I never told her what they watched. It would have upset her. Dad would poke fun at me, point to the screen, and encourage me to stay and watch. I fled to my Nana, but another relative did stay and this relative went on to allegedly sexually assault another relative. I firmly put the blame for that on my parents. Those vile videos should never have come into our house. Dad was a bus driver and would often do the Aberdeen to London routes, so I guess that's where he got them from. He would boast on his return about new ones.

It was at this time that my clothes were not getting washed, and I wasn't permitted to bathe or shower. I smelt. The shame of having other school children telling me I have stunk of urine has stayed with me into adulthood.

My gentle therapist would reinforce to me it wasn't my fault, what my parents did was not normal, and she told me, time and time again, that I didn't smell in her small office. Even now I liberally spray on the anti-perspirant and aftershave and love a daily bath.

When I am asked about my childhood, the memories that I share are all based around being at Nana's and Grandad's. I rarely talk about being at the house where my parents lived. When Karla and I were dating, we would spend most of our leave at her home in Woodbridge, Suffolk, and return to Aberdeen to see my Nana and Grandad. We stayed with my parents and by this time; they had stopped beating me and were nice to me in front of Karla. When my grandparents died, it broke my heart, and we stopped returning to Aberdeen. I was a student nurse when Nana passed, and my army nurse tutors allowed me leave to go to her funeral. Grandad passed several years later, and I was not permitted leave because the wards were too busy at the tri-service Royal Hospital Haslar in Gosport. That hurt a lot.

Years later, when our children were young, we moved back to Aberdeenshire because I missed living in Scotland. My parents had aged, and I thought they might have changed, but it wasn't to be, no matter how hard we tried with them. They just didn't seem to show interest in our children's lives. They refused invitations to attend school plays and wouldn't turn up at arranged times to take them to karate. Karla and I stopped asking, and the children showed little interest in relatives who didn't seem to care for them. I was relieved. I didn't want them beating my children like they had me.

I had some aunties and uncles, and my favourite was my auntie, Carol. After visiting Nana, I would pop in and see her and my cousin Helen. My favourite memories are of us all having Sunday lunches at Nana's. Then I'd tend the garden, and, in the winter, I would paint windowsills and skirting boards. But my mum put a stop to it because she didn't want the other family members thinking she didn't feed me at home. Though I got beaten for it, I would continue to visit my grandparents whenever I could. It wasn't about the food for me; it was about feeling loved and wanted.

As an example of my parents' behaviour, I was engrossed in playing The Hobbit on my Spectrum 48K computer; it was all the rage in the

1980s. Dad came into my bedroom and took his belt to me because I was using the electric and the meter was zooming around. I fled to Nana's and rarely played computer games again.

Be prepared to talk about your childhood and share what is uppermost in your mind with your therapist. Once we understand our early years, we can enjoy our later years that much more.

CHAPTER 46:

MARRIAGE AND RELATIONSHIPS

Your relationship with those closest to you will inevitably be affected by PTSD and grief. We are only human after all and come with all our own emotional baggage. Life and all your emotions aren't paused because of your medical condition or when someone you love dies. That's why counsellors, psychologists and psychotherapists will gently talk about your loved ones, how they affect your moods and day-to-day living. It certainly played a factor in my journey of healing. Losing a child and developing any long-term disability will put an enormous strain on any relationship.

I met Karla when we were eighteen. We sat next to each other in nursing classes. A friendship grew and then we became boyfriend and girlfriend and were engaged to be married about a year later. We had a blast! We explored the local areas of wherever we were posted, enjoyed going out for meals and to the cinema. We did most tourist attractions like the Tower of London, Alton Towers and zoos and wildlife parks. We laughed and had fun.

We wed at twenty-one, soon after I qualified as a Registered General Nurse. Karla was ill several times during parts of her training and was moved back a few groups to enable her to recommence her training. The first Gulf War also interrupted her training, as it did many army student nurses. I was more fortunate as I was weeks away from qualifying, so it was decided that our group could sit our final exams. We all passed, despite this added pressure.

It was idyllic at the hospitals we worked and learned in as students. Despite being in segregated accommodation, we practically lived in each other's rooms – sorry Matron! Though we were once caught snuggled up together, fortunately fully dressed, watching TV, by the Company Sergeant Major! We didn't half get a bollocking! We made sure to always leave one side of the huge locker wardrobes empty so that the illegal visitor could jump in and hide if anyone tried to come into our rooms again – and we learnt to keep the door locked.

When we were posted apart, we always spent days off together and tried to get our annual leave to coincide. Though Karla had a lot of sick time as she struggled to cope with the challenges of what happened to her as a child. This caused a lot of turbulence in our lives after we were married and learnt new roles. It could often be stormy when there were the added pressures of bringing up children, trying to earn a wage while forging careers in the military and then as civilian nurses. It wasn't easy, especially when Karla would take herself off her prescribed medicines or outright refuse her GPs to keep me informed. Even when she was hospitalised in psychiatric wards with a twenty-four-hour watch with a nurse or carer wherever she went, she wouldn't allow anyone, not even herself, to keep me informed. It was tough for me, but more for Karla as she battled her demons and attempted suicide.

I had my lovely, faithful dog, Bessie, to keep me sane, and the years between her having to be put down and not having my adorable Lynne, were lonely and painful.

In the early years of trying to cope with our grief, Karla, Abigail, and I went to various support groups and retreats held by grief charities. That peer support helped enormously, especially seeing that other parents and siblings could go on with their lives, albeit in a new way, while carrying their grief and various emotions. What I found sad was the number of marriages and close relationships that crumbled. Some admitted that the relationships were floundering anyway, and the death tipped it over the edge. Others couldn't cope with the pointing of blame that inevitably comes with any loss.

In the early days of losing Angus to suicide, I would rack my brain wondering why and if I was at fault. Was it the way I brought him up? Did I support him enough? But then we discovered his torn first draft suicide letter, and I knew there was only one person to blame for his suicide and that was the perpetrator of the crime against Angus.

I can't imagine how difficult it must be to stay in a relationship where someone thinks you are to blame for the death. I am minded of one person I met whose child confided they would take their own life. This parent did not take their child to a place of safety and laughed off the comment. The child died within the hour and was found the next day. The guilt must be an unbearable burden.

Losing a child can bring some relationships closer together but also tear them apart.

When I entered my care package to help with my demons, the subject of Karla came up each time. Over many sessions, I was made to see just how difficult Karla's mood swings and verbal outbursts had been and how they had demoralised me over the years. As much as I love her, she was difficult to live with. When she takes her medicines and follows the advice of her care workers, psychiatrist, and GP, she's a delight to be with, but those years before were challenging. But it's the same for any relationship – there will be bumps on the road. The key to success is open and frank communication. That said, the tables turned, and poor Karla had to cope with my temper outbursts as I tried to understand my PTSD and what was going on in my head. It was her turn to encourage me to take my prescribed medicines and seek various treatments.

I've learnt to take my medicines to keep me at my best. During the periods where Karla has had excellent treatment and followed a care plan, we have had a happy marriage and were blessed with Angus and Abigail. My canine Mistresses, Bessie, and Lynne have kept me on the straight and narrow and though Karla jokes they were and are my Mistresses, deep down, she knows I need a dog in my life to provide companionship and support.

The psychiatric talking therapies have helped me come to terms with my lost employment and I've made peace with myself that it was the best decision to forego my nursing career to ensure Karla's safety and to bring up the children. The psychologist and counsellors brought much peace to my mind, especially the emotional pain of losing Angus and discovering what happened to him. I would urge anyone in similar circumstances to seek professional help from a counsellor, psychotherapist or psychologist or read the meditation chapter and approach a suitable organisation. Above all, keep talking and be honest. The best marriages and partnerships are those that are honest and open with each other. Most of all, be honest with yourself. If you find yourself in a toxic relationship, it could be the time to take the advice of friends and family and leave that person and concentrate on taking better care of yourself. Read the shedding excess baggage chapter for my thoughts.

CHAPTER 47:

DIET

You owe it to yourself and those you love to follow a healthy diet. I don't advocate starving yourself until you are stick thin, but to follow the latest science and health advice. Currently, the NHS advocates a high-protein and plant diet which is low in fat and sugars. Such sugars include refined, and those found in fruits like berries and apples. The occasional piece of fruit as a treat is fine, but I'm afraid you'll have to put away those chocolate bars.

For the first three days after Angus took his life, Karla and I ate little. Then our poo turned liquid green. I kid you not. Mine was like something out of Doctor Who. We both told the other that we ought to eat, but neither of us felt like eating, or doing much for that matter. Then our dear friend Sandra came round with a beef pie and a fruit pudding from the local farm shop. Both looked so tempting and our fasts were broken. Then we took to eating all the wrong things. Crisps, sweets, chocolate, all the lovely shiny things from the local supermarkets. We needed those sugar highs to see us through the days and nights of grief. Our weight ballooned. I put on almost two stones and at my stage of life, it's hard to lose it. This went on for years until I had routine bloods taken and the doctor told me my cholesterol was high and my liver function tests were all over the place. She told me I was at risk of a heart attack or stroke. Then I thought of Abigail. She needed her daft old dad. I decided to lose weight and get fitter.

Lots of exercise is out of the question because of my painful lower legs, probably caused by too many army boot runs, stretcher races and carrying far too much kit on my back on exercises. Thanks, army! Though it was fun at the time.

I followed my GP's advice and dieted. My bloods are getting better results and I feel so much more alert and less lethargic. I gave up the sweets that I would treat myself to whenever I was typing away at the computer.

I thought I was eating healthy by munching on bananas and apples, three of each a day, along with a bowl of strawberries and grapes. But they were packed full of sugar. I was surreptitiously getting my sugar high again. Salads became my friend, along with lots of porridge oats (none of the ready stuff -it's full of syrup and sugar) for breakfast or eggs, spinach, and mushrooms. I'm hopeless at making omelettes and Karla calls these my concoctions. They turn out like scrambled eggs, but I find them filing and tasty. I may even enter MasterChef one day! She shattered that illusion by buying me an electric omelette maker!

I try to not eat meat at least one day a week. I cook vegetarian curries from scratch using ingredients like marrow or aubergines. Their consistency is like eating meat.

We reduced our portion sizes and try to aim for only 2500 to 1900 calories for me and 2000 for Karla each day. The NHS app told us she needs less than me – she wasn't too pleased! I use the calculator on my phone and tap in the calorie count of whatever I eat. I use a search engine to find out the scores, though most packets, tins, etc. have the calories on the label and can be easily worked out. Try to avoid foods with the red and amber colours of the contents. The greens are ideal in the handy food traffic light scoring.

My Body Mass Index rose to 32, which put me in the obese category. There is a handy NHS BMI calculator online, and I tracked my weight loss through it and quickly lost a few pounds over two weeks, then a pound of weight fell off me most weeks until I slunk to the overweight category. Now I hover around 24, which puts me smugly in the higher echelon of the normal weight bracket for my height, but I still need to lose some more weight to get my bloods to acceptable levels.

We have tried to cut out any junk food from our diet. We switched from white bread, rice, and pasta to the occasional wholewheat bread and pasta and only cook with brown rice. These minor changes help keep our weight down and are easily made. We swapped potatoes in favour of sweet potato, which also counts as one of your five a day portion.

As a treat, we sometimes eat dark chocolate, which has been proven to lower cholesterol, so long as you only eat one square. The higher the cocoa percentage, the better, though it tastes bitter compared to the high sugar content of milk chocolate.

Avocados are two portions of your five a day vegetable and are a low sugar fruit. Ideally, we should aim for eight to ten portions of vegetables a day. I love mushrooms and spinach and now lettuce and celery, so that's easy. Avocados have also been shown to reduce cholesterol. So have red grapefruits, though the sugars are high in these, so I only have the occasional one.

Turkey is the best low-fat meat and is great in stir-fries. Lynne loves the skin from this and chicken and gets them as an occasional treat. We try to avoid processed foods like bacon and sausages and have them only when we stay somewhere overnight and have an inclusive breakfast. If there is a buffet, most of my meat gets chopped up into Lynne's special Tupperware tub. She salivates when she sees me take it out. She's very Pavlovian! You watch her whenever I have a treat in my hand. She always licks her lips in anticipation. Just as she has learnt my body language, I've a deep understanding of her body language and can anticipate most of her actions and needs. We are a great double act, though I know her understanding of our partnership is that I'm a food dispenser!

I miss a takeaway though! But all those saturated fats, the ones that taste so great in pizzas, curries and haggis and chips from the chipper, were not doing my cholesterol levels any good and they certainly weren't doing my mental health any favours, there really is truth in the phrase, 'Healthy body, healthy mind.' Though sometimes I give into temptation and order one in.

There is even mindfulness in eating. I do this most days. I chew my food slowly, savouring each mouthful, enjoying the texture and taste. I smell the food and often hold it. I enjoy the stillness and peace of eating. That's the five senses technique we explored in an earlier chapter.

Chewing and taking your time also trick the mind into feeling full. Scientists have discovered the brain doesn't know your stomach is full until twenty minutes after eating. By taking this length of time to eat, you can quickly lose weight.

Putting your meals onto smaller plates also tricks the mind into thinking you have a larger portion. The NHS recommends this and has the research to back it.

I was a grazer and enjoyed a large snack in the evenings. I blamed my anti-depressants – there was that old denial again. But really, I was comfort eating. I have swapped the nuts and sweets for batons of carrots, (Lynne loves the peelings and they are good for clearing her anal glands) and strips of celery. Though I've gradually phased out eating in the late-night hours now after learning about time restricted eating. TRE is fasting that signals to your body to break down the fats. It's easy to do this by stopping eating as early in the evening as you can, fasting overnight whilst you are sleeping, then having your breakfast as late as possible. No calories should be digested at all, not even milk in your tea or coffee, nor fizzy or sports drinks. The higher the ratio, the better. I have mine at 15:9 based on the 24-hour clock, because I stop eating at 7pm and start again at 10am. I work from home, so can eat breakfast as late as possible. If you work, try having your breakfast at lunch or during your mid-morning break. The body soon sheds fat while maintaining muscle from your proteins. My next stage is to stop eating by 6pm so that my ratio becomes 16:8. Begin with a ratio of 12:12, then escalate the fasting time. I noticed an improvement in mental clarity and fewer digestion problems because my body wasn't having to work hard breaking down what I put into it. My sleep was improved as well, for the same reasons. Dizzy feelings can be overcome by drinking lots of water.

We now do online shopping, which stops me going Thermonuclear and bed-ridden, but it also has the added advantage that we don't impulse buy. Watch out for those naughty, enticing two for one offers. We only order in what we need for each carefully thought-out meal, with the occasional treat. Those adverts on the telly put temptations into our minds as we write out the shopping list. But that's okay, the occasional treat does you good.

Try to make some of these simple changes and have a think about your eating choices and weight.

CHAPTER 48:

PSYCHIC MEDIUMS

At the first appointment with my regular GP, which was within days of losing Angus to suicide, she said a strange thing. She warned us not to approach psychic mediums. Karla and I were in the room together. I was too unwell to go alone. We looked at each other, and our doctor must have seen our puzzled faces. She explained one was working in the area, preying on the vulnerable and she has had to deal with the aftermath.

Obituaries in the local newspapers help the mediums to target the recently bereaved, and social media must aid in their research. In our area, which has a strong fishing heritage, the custom is for funeral notices to be placed in newsagents, grocery shops and Post Offices. It must be a great help to mediums working the area.

I'd like to give you the same warning – don't be tempted to seek the services of anyone who claims to be clairvoyant or a psychic. They are charlatans. I've been around the dead long enough to know they don't communicate from beyond the grave. I only wish they did. I'd love to hear from Angus and my grandparents again. As I'm sure you would love to hear from your loved ones too. There would be so much to say, starting with, 'I love you, and miss you.' Death, particularly a sudden one, like in battle, or by suicide or accident, leaves so many unanswered questions. I'm afraid you will have to accept they won't go answered.

It will tear you up. It'll make you scream and cry. You'll have lots of anger and sorrow, perhaps you'll strike up a bargain with God – just don't go anywhere near these fraudsters.

They will fill your head with nonsense and damaging words. They are good at understanding body language; they do their research, then they pounce. They may tell you what you want to hear, but it'll come at a cost to your mental health. Ignore their tarot cards, tea leaf reading and crystal ball and walk away. Don't let them in if they ring the doorbell or telephone you. You may think you'll gain comfort from hearing from your loved one once again, but it isn't them.

If you need validation that your loved one is at peace, in heaven, turn to the church for solace, but not to a spiritual church. They are the worst fraudsters. Padres, vicars, ministers, and their laypeople can help ease your anguish and set you right. Our local minister was a former army chaplain and provided comfort to Karla, though now she doesn't go to church, except with me on Remembrance Day.

We avoided psychic mediums for about six months, then one came into our lives in the most unlikely of places.

We were in a church hall, attending a bereavement support group for those who had been affected by suicide. It was held monthly, and this was the fifth time we'd attended. The group facilitator seemed an amiable lady. In this meeting, at Christmas time, she introduced her son, who had attended no meetings before, as the new facilitator. The other regulars, who had been attending meetings for years, looked shocked. Then, over coffee, I found out why. He worked the room.

This new facilitator, of a group of vulnerable people, went from person to person, talking about his services as a psychic medium. In my case, he told me he could cure my PTSD through past-life regression. I was stunned as he told me about several military men he 'treated.' They'd fought in Iraq and Afghanistan, and he claimed to have cured them of their PTSD by taking them back to their former lives. He boasted about weaning them off their medication. I was aghast and could only think about the amount of damage he'd caused to their mental health. He certainly wasn't qualified to be fiddling with medication.

He told me about his office, a few streets away, and how I could come for tarot readings, or to speak to Angus, through him. I wondered if he was going to have the gall to give me a business card. I was about to tell him what I thought of his services when he then moved onto his next victim. I found out later that he did indeed give out business cards to members of our group.

I wonder if such people have an undiagnosed mental health condition and I wish they would seek professional help. Then they won't be damaging other people's frail mental states.

Karla was angry when we chatted later, and we were perplexed about what we should do. This man could do untold damage to fragile minds, including ours.

Fortunately, the decision was taken from me by my fantastic doctor. When she asked about the support group, I explained what had happened and how we probably wouldn't return. She looked shocked and I think angry too. She said, 'Leave it with me.'

She, rightly, ensuring the welfare of her patients, phoned the charity and warned them of what was happening. They took immediate action. The facilitator and her son were never seen again at any meeting. Though she sent an e-mail stating that her son does a lot of good by healing people and helping them. He didn't. I soon deleted the e-mail and moved on.

The support group dynamics changed. No longer did the facilitator talk over people. Each person was heard and given solace and advice. It transpired that the old facilitator was stopping deputies from being trained and was chairing meetings throughout Scotland. I suspect her son went too, offering his fraudulent services.

Please stay well clear of these people. Your loved one is at rest and cannot, sadly, communicate with you. Don't line these charlatans' pockets. Instead, use the money to pay for a qualified counsellor, psychotherapist, or psychologist. Ironically, these fully trained professional fees are usually lower than what these so-called mediums and clairvoyants outrageously charge.

CHAPTER 49:

SEEING AND TALKING
TO THE DEAD

During psychotherapy, the psychologist asked me a strange question. 'Do you talk to Angus?'

I replied, 'No. He's dead.'

She patiently described how some of her patients find solace in speaking aloud to their lost loved one. Some do this throughout the day, others when sat in front of their photograph. Think of the widow, in my novel, One Last War, who picks up a framed photo of her long-gone husband from her bedside, and chats about the day she had. Maybe it's not so odd now.

I haven't done this, but it could be something that you draw comfort from. I guess it may even help you work through issues, like with a silent counsellor.

It wouldn't be odd to see someone stand or kneel by a graveside and talk to the headstone or down to the earth where the deceased rests in peace. So why should it be odd to see someone go about their day while having a one-sided conversation with a missed loved one? Grief affects us all differently and we should not judge their grieving process.

I knew from my nursing days that many people say they saw their dead relative soon after their death or funeral. They said how reassuring it made them feel. None spoke of fright.

Could it be that they willed their lost loved one to appear at the foot of their bed? I've never seen Angus and in a cruel twist, I see the dead I have cared for instead. A cuddle with Lynne soon chases them away. I find them frightening and I wish they would leave me alone.

During a holiday, I met a former Royal Marine who was asking me about my PTSD. I explained about the flashbacks and nightmares. He thought they weren't flashbacks, but were spirits trying to communicate with me. Karla soon put him right! It transpired that he was a preacher in his local spiritual church. He didn't speak to us again during the holiday when Karla told him about how we lost Angus and didn't believe in the ethos of his church. I often wonder about his mental health and the harm his organisation may be doing.

When Nana died, it seemed like I saw her everywhere, but it was only women who looked like her, from a distance. I think my mind was playing tricks and was willing for her to show herself. Years later, when I was recovering from a hernia operation that encountered complications, I saw my Nana and both Granddads. They were waving to me from a distance, but when I tried to walk to them, in this dream, they shooed me away. Then they waved goodbye and were gone. I could not physically walk to them because of the pain. I was also bedbound, hooked up to a drip, catheterised, and dopey from medicines. Perhaps they were there, willing me to get better, or maybe it was all a drug-induced dream. Whichever it was, I drew great comfort from seeing them happy together. I wished I could have been with them and would have engaged in conversation and hugged them.

When Angus took his life, wherever I went, I saw happy sons with their fathers. I wished I could go back in time and relive the happy times we had together. It hurt to see what they had and what I could never have again. Though I have happy memories, they don't bring my dear boy back.

When Bessie, my beautiful flat-coated retriever, was put down because of failing health, every dog I saw thereafter was a flat-coat. Yet, before this, they were rare in our area.

If it brings you solace, then speak to your dead friend or relative. If you are lucky enough to see them again, then cherish the moment.

CHAPTER 50:

ILLEGAL DRUGS, ALCOHOL AND SMOKING

Just don't! When I developed PTSD, I did what many military folks did. I turned to alcohol to get the images out of head and to help me get to sleep and hope my nightmares wouldn't seek a way through my drunken state. It didn't work, and it brings its own problems, like impaired judgement and gastric issues. It'll also affect your social circles and could affect your relationships. You will inevitably act out of character.

I wouldn't drink too heavily in front of Karla. I feigned an interest in malt whisky so that I'd have an excuse to slip a bottle into the shopping trolley, along with cans of lager or bottles of ale. I even pretended to show an interest in the ale labels, but what I was really doing was looking for the strongest.

I'd pour a generous dram or two of whisky into the pint glass. If Karla left the home during the day, I'd crack open the lager or cider, often mixing the two into a glass to make a snakebite. Then I'd have to finish both cans and open more.

I did the tricks of sucking on mints to disguise the smell of alcohol or swirling round some mouthwash.

I let Karla drive. She was more able then. It gave me an opportunity to drink throughout the day.

It contributed to my weight gain. There were hidden calories in the ales and lagers.

Karla needs more sleep than me, so when she went to bed early, I would pour generous drams of my favourite malts. When I rose earlier than her, I would take the bottles to the bin or walk to the recycling point a few streets away.

When I did the shopping on my own, I would stock up again and squirrel the bottles and cans away in the furthest corners of the cupboard.

None of this helped get the images out of my mind, nor those playing out all around me like a macabre video game. I still woke myself up crying out from nightmares.

I took to carrying a hip flask in my jacket pocket so I could have a swig or three whenever I was away from home.

I gave up alcohol several years ago. The PTSD medicines I finally got from my understanding GP made me ill if I took them while drinking. I don't miss it. The drugs are much more effective at dampening down my PTSD. I'm more alert throughout the day and function better. I miss the taste of Drambuie, though. I must confess that I still have a bottle of it in the cupboard and sometimes I tease the cork out and give the contents a good sniff, just for old times' sake!

I will not admit to taking illegal drugs. I don't want bother from the police again! What I will say is if you are taking them to help you cope with your grief or PTSD, it isn't a long-term solution to a natural process, nor is it good for your treatment of a medical condition. Go to your GP instead and talk openly about your health and feelings. If they won't help, then go to another until you find one that understands you and will help treat you.

Long-term usage of drugs like cannabis brings its own problems and you have enough going on with your life. It can lead to dark depressions, anger, and paranoia, symptoms you may already have.

Don't make them worse by taking illicit substances.

Nor is it safe to put your life in the hands of the local drug dealer. Put it in the hands of your local doctor instead. I have to say that the effects of getting drunk I now experience from the combination of legal medicines I take. I wait until my eyelids are so heavy and my vision gets blurry before going to bed. Then it is lights out for several blissful hours. My mind shuts down and I don't recall those nightmares. Then I rise when I'm more alert. This seems to lessen my exposure to vivid nightmares. When Karla's not around, I often have an afternoon nap in my armchair, with Lynne curled up beside me. She loves a good nap too! We are so suited. Then when my nightmares start, I stop napping and get back to work in the study or have a play with Lynne. She is learning scent work and soon sniffs out the hidden tin with a few drops of gun oil. This will then lead onto her sniffing out a rag or t-shirt which has been exposed to the sweats I get when I have nightmares. Then, in time, she will recognise the smell I exude at the start of a nightmare and wake me up. I won't miss her sticking her tongue down my throat! Instead, she'll be trained to nudge me awake with her nose. She's a clever girl, my Lynne.

I've never smoked cigarettes or cigars, though as a child I liked to puff on those liquorice pipes – remember them! They were ever so tasty. As a child of the 70s and 80s, it seems ludicrous now that sweet manufacturers could sell treats that children could use to mimic smoking. Chocolate cigarettes even came in attractive boxes, and the thin paper they were wrapped in could also be eaten. I'm pleased they are no longer made, as later in life, I saw the damage smoking does to the human body. I've nursed people, frightened people, who gasped for breath, and struggled to oxygenate their body because of their addictions. I've held the hand of dying patients as they took their last breath at a premature age all because of the cancer that ate away at their body, often reducing themselves to half and sometimes a quarter of their former selves.

I hope to see a total ban on nicotine in my lifetime because it robs people of their loved ones. I often wonder if it is why my dear Nana was taken from me at such an early age. She had Chronic Obstructive Pulmonary Disease because of years of smoking. When I was growing up, I would see her struggle for breath. She often had a wheeze and was on many inhalers and devices to deliver much-needed medicines to her lungs. She died, alone, and suddenly, from heart failure. It broke my heart and I miss her to this day. Please spare your loved ones this heartache and give up this addiction. It's not a coping mechanism for stress or anxiety, it's a killer.

Your local GP surgery will help enormously to wean you off the cigarettes, vaping, cigars, etc. There is also help from nearby chemists. Treatment plans are available for free from the NHS. It is never too late to stem or reverse the damage smoking does to your body.

Find your own solution to get you off illegal drugs, alcohol, and cease smoking. Be honest with yourself and those close to you. Book another appointment with your GP and seek their help in coming safely off these substances. They won't mind. They would rather you led a healthier lifestyle.

CHAPTER 51:

HUMOUR IN GRIEF AND PTSD

It's not all doom and gloom when you experience grief and develop PTSD. You may not see it, but humour is there and helps keep your sanity. That's why people who experience the worst of humanity, like police officers and nurses, often have the sickest and darkest of humour. Gallows humour it could be described as. I certainly have it in double-doses – from my army and nursing background.

The bizarreness of grief started at the police mortuary. We were shown into the narrow waiting room with curtains in front of us and to the side. The nervous police liaison officer said we should prepare ourselves to see Angus through a window, and that his face was an odd colour because of the method of suicide. She said she'd give us a minute to settle before pulling the curtain apart. I hadn't the heart to tell her the curtains didn't meet and there was a gap you could drive a tank through. I could see Angus clearly through this gap. I needed the chair that was behind me as I sat and fully realised that this was real. The police officers who came to our house in the early hours hadn't made a mistake. The phrase, 'My world fell apart,' doesn't even start to cover it. Nothing can prepare you for seeing your child laid out on a trolley, with the typical purple cloth covering them up to their neck.

The police officer then said she'd excuse herself while we had a few minutes with Angus and that there were tissues on the table. As she left, I turned to take a tissue, but the table was bare. Much like my heart and soul felt.

Registering Angus's death at the Aberdeenshire Council office brought its own humour, or lack of, unfortunately. The Registrar I spoke to on the phone was sympathetic and offered words of kind succour as we agreed a time to go there to receive death certificates. The waiting room was full of happy mums and dads, proudly fussing over their newborns, eagerly about to register their births. Amongst this sunshine, our dark clouds descended.

We were soon shown into a room by a stern, headmistress-like woman who offered no words of condolence. Her manner was brisk, and she batted away any help from the other kindly Registrar and even read out Angus's cause of death and injuries whilst poring over the post-mortem report, which was also read aloud. Abigail was with us and I'd been trying for days to save her from this information. Noting that the post-mortem had not been signed by the doctor performing his autopsy, she tutted, told us in no uncertain terms that we couldn't register his death until this was so, then, in front of us, phoned the mortuary and demanded to speak to the medical officer. She proceeded to have a conversation with the person who had cut my son open. We had to wait, in stony silence, until an electronic signature was relayed to the Registrar. Fortunately, the kindly Registrar stopped what she was doing and came across to offer comforting words to Abigail and Karla. Another example of Aberdeenshire Council failing my family. I wonder about the level of training their personnel receive. I hope this Registrar moved onto another department or job, preferably with no human contact. In nursing, such nurses with the same attitude to people would often levitate to work in theatres where their patients are oblivious to such brashness, thanks to being anaesthetised!

The oddities continued to follow us like a faithful dog at the funeral parlour. The funeral director talked over us, boasted about his history in the local area, of how he built his business and ignored our requests. He even tutted as we made decision after decision, diligently answering his tick list of questions. Then he rushed off, biding us to follow him. He shouted through to his colleagues as we passed the treatment room, where I saw a pair of feet on the ceramic table. They looked young, and I guessed they were Angus's. A hand appeared and clutched the door from the other side, like in a ham Hammer Horror film from the seventies. It slowly closed the door with a creak. Then the director showed us into a room. We stepped into a large area filled with assorted coffins. I half expected someone to come out of one, like Dracula rising. We were encouraged to choose one, like we were in a sweetie shop deciding between marshmallows or toffee.

Weirdness even dogged me at the Combat Stress assessment. I'd written at length on the forms about how I now find helicopters and jets an overwhelming sight. As I was ushered into a room, I spied the exact helicopter I had entered to retrieve the aircrew bodies adorning the wall. Its framed neighbours were of smiling loadmasters and jet crew, alongside, you've guessed it, photos of Tornado jets. I stuttered and asked the psychiatric nurse if it was a test. It wasn't. I stripped as many layers as I could as I sweated through the interview, my thermonuclear state going off the scale. I left the room a gibbering wreck.

Months later, I received a letter from Police Scotland stating that I could now have the laptop and mobile phone they had taken from Angus's flat. I was told to take this letter to the reception of Fraserburgh Police Station. I knew the way. I'd been mugshot and fingerprinted there earlier in the year. The letter clearly stated that Angus had died from suicide and that I could now retrieve my deceased son's belongings.

I duly took the letter to the stern receptionist, whose lack of a smile could give the funeral director a run for his money. She faithfully read it, word for word in a few long minutes, and uttered the appalling sentence, 'Do you have the permission of your son?'

No humour could penetrate my grief. I was dumbfounded and told her, 'No. He is dead.'

Without missing a heartbeat, nor pausing for breath, she said in a calm voice, 'I'll just get them.'

She returned and wordlessly handed over the items the police had analysed as part of their investigation. This was mostly paperwork from his flat, along with his mobile phone and laptop.

It wasn't funny at the time, but now I look back on it and laugh. I hope you do too. I think Angus would have laughed his socks off!

The laptop and phone had been reset to factory settings; all files erased. They provided no answers and gave us another question to think about. Did Angus or the police do this?

Wanting to escape from the neighbourhood noises that were intruding on our grief, Karla and I took Abigail to the cinema in Aberdeen. We used to go there once a week and would see several films in one day with a break for an enjoyable meal at one of the beach restaurants or cafes. We chose a Naomie Harris and Will Smith film, two fine actors, so I thought it would be good. It had us in tears and distressed Abigail. It was called Collateral Beauty and was about a man who lost a child, and then his mind. It struck home with me and has the most wonderful twist that I didn't see coming. It was also proof to me we could not escape our grief and had to tackle it head on and, somehow, forge a new life for ourselves. It's a beautiful film, and I'd encourage you to grab a box of tissues and sit down to watch it.

Don't feel bad about laughing again. It took me months to get my humour back. Embrace it. Humour is a great healer and coping mechanism.

CHAPTER 52:

AT LEAST

I don't find any humour in the "At least" brigade. I want to give them a good slap. I'm not normally a violent man, but I imagine knocking sense into them. There are no "At least" platitudes in grief. It offers me no comfort to be told, "Well, at least you had him for twenty-two years." I want to shake these people and yell, "But I wanted him for more than that. I should not have outlived him. That's the natural order of things. I should have died first. He should have been at my funeral." Life is as cruel as these remarks and, sadly, there are people out there who have said such things to Karla and me.

Perhaps I'm being a little unfair. Maybe these people meant well, but have had no experience of grief and don't know how to talk to people in mourning. It's easy for me to forget that I've had a lot of training in grief and loss from my nursing background. I've read a lot about it as a clinician and latterly as a father seeking help and looking for answers. If you fall into this category, the greatest gift you can give to someone mourning is your time and a listening ear. You really don't have to say much. Simply sit or walk with them. Ignore the impulse to blurt out words you hope will comfort. Place a reassuring hand on their shoulder, embrace them or hold their hand. Give them the comfort of a friend. Simply be with them.

Grief and PTSD are not games of top trumps. There are no winners. The one with the highest card value doesn't win. No matter how long that person was in your life for, from in the womb, as a baby, a toddler, a teenager, or an adult child, it is still a catastrophic loss and everyone will grieve differently and at their own pace. Please don't compare this loss with others, as some well-meaning people have said to me. I really have had to hold back and bite my tongue. Fortunately, for every crass individual, there are hundreds of folk who know how to say the right thing, or do the most natural thing in the world and offer support. I am minded of a lady, who could see I was struggling at a funeral tea. It was the first funeral I'd attended since Angus's and the loud, crowded room was causing me some issues. This was before I had my lovely Lynne. The wonderful lady, who I hardly knew, simply sat, and held my hand. It calmed me and reassured me while Karla was with her friend. Be that lady.

CHAPTER 53:

DRIVING

I once lent my car to Abigail so she could get to university on time for a lecture. I never drove it again! She laid claim to it and even renamed it! I didn't mind. My driving, at that stage in my suicidal desires, was shocking. I would take risk after risk, not caring if I hurt someone, hoping I'd hurt myself. I don't really mean hurt. I mean kill myself.

I was worse after coffee. It made me wired and thoughtless.

I wasn't a horn blaster. Nor was I a middle finger sticker in the air and I didn't road rage anyone. But I tailgated. I got shockingly close to other cars, willing them to move out of the lane so I could go faster. Karla would sit there, in her motability car, white knuckled against the dashboard. Her feet pumping down on imaginary brakes.

Then a change in my thought behaviour happened about halfway through psychotherapy. I worried about other drivers and pedestrians. It was a sign that I was healing. I was worrying about others. That old nurse in me was resurfacing. I slowed down and became more thoughtful on the roads.

I've learnt not to drive after taking my Pregabalin. I wait for an hour or two for the floaty sensation to wear off. Instead, I go into the garden with Lynne, and we play her go find it game where I hide treats and she sniffs them out. We sit in the arbour. I enjoy a hot peach sugar-free squash and we watch my white doves fly around and go back safely into their shed. We observe the wild birds' flitter between feeders and dart and frolic. This keeps me away from the car and is a great mindfulness moment to start the day.

My concentration levels took a pounding after developing PTSD and in my grief. They've never fully recovered, but I have adapted. I don't drive more than a few hours at the most. Even then, it is broken into forty-minute chunks and then I rest, either by taking Lynne for a nearby stroll, or having a snack in a café. When I go to Bravehound HQ, I will drive the day before and stay in a Travelodge or dog-friendly guesthouse. When I return home, I'll stay an extra night so that I can set off after a nutritious breakfast and having taken my drugs prior to the meal and packing the car.

Several of my friends who also have PTSD have given up their car because their flashbacks have been too severe, and it was affecting their driving. This is a sensible approach.

Think about your own driving safety and the impact it has on others. Consider other means of transport or asking your partner or a friend to take the wheel.

CHAPTER 54:

SHORT-TERM GOALS

My thoughts about the future died when Angus did. It was a catastrophic loss. As a father, I wanted the best for my children, and my hopes and aspirations were for them.

It pleases me to see Abigail with a loving partner, in a secure job, volunteering on the phones at ChildLine, having a close circle of friends and training towards being a counsellor.

For myself, I can't see a future beyond the next day. It's enough for me to get out of bed and enjoy the day with Lynne by my side. I hope we have many happy years together. I don't dream of holidays or owning a flash car or living in a larger house. The thought of not being able to take Lynne on holiday and being without her mortifies me. Besides, there are enough celebrities hosting travel programs on the telly and I can vicariously get my holiday fix through them. Perhaps one day we'll venture into other parts of the UK together. There are enough walks in our stunning village and around the Aberdeenshire coast to satisfy us both.

I don't have any career aspirations, though I hope this book will be favourably received and get nice 5-star reviews at Amazon and Good Reads. I love writing. Exploring my feelings and experiences has been therapeutic, and it's nice when someone contacts me to say how much pleasure they got from reading my novels. I have planned a series of novels around The Fence, my military post-apocalyptic zombie survival adventure. It's fun creating new ways to kill the infected!

I want the quiet life now. I've seen enough bloodshed, death, and trauma to last me a lifetime. I pray Abigail leads a full, happy, and healthy life.

However, I find it helpful to have short-term goals. That's all I can concentrate on now. Currently, this is clearing out the big shed and the loft and listing things on eBay or throwing them out. Decorating is also filling my thoughts. But that's it. I have little in the way of career aspirations, other than to bring pleasure to people through my books.

Perhaps this may help you too. Living with PTSD is a daily struggle. Coping with grief is hard, terribly hard. It may be enough for you to get out of bed, function through the day and have as best a sleep as you can. I hope this book helps. Just concentrate on short-term goals. Then one day, you might think a month or year ahead, perhaps even two or three.

When Angus passed away by suicide, I didn't think I'd get past five minutes. Then I developed full-on PTSD, and I didn't think I'd live past five hours. But I sought help, all of which is described in this self-help, autobiographical book. Then I saw myself living past five days, just to get to a healthcare appointment. Then the military charities that offered free holidays helped me get to see beyond five weeks. Soundproofing my home and receiving noise-cancelling headphones from Help for Heroes got me through five months. The support and advice from Bravehound made me see living beyond five years. Being lucky enough to be matched with Lynne makes me realise how wonderful life is and I know I'll make it to another decade, with her by my side every step of the way.

Set yourself one realistic short-term goal. Discuss it with your family and friends. You could even post it as a visitor post on my Facebook page at www.facebook.com/cgbuswell or let me know at www.cgbuswell.com/contact.php

Find your one thing that will get you beyond five minutes, then gradually build up to hours, days, weeks, months and maybe even years.

CHAPTER 55:

FIREWORKS

When I left the army, Karla, the children, and I settled in the town of Woodbridge. It's a delightful area of Suffolk with a picturesque windmill and stunning walks along the River Deben. Our terraced house was built in the 1930s for the employees of British Rail. The previous owner had built a rear extension, and we had a vast garden. There was a Chinese takeaway five doors away. Whenever Bessie went out to the garden, she'd stop, raise her nose in the air, and have a good sniff to see what was on the menu. I often did the same!

But their family let off fireworks every Bonfire Night, our New Year's Eve and for the Chinese New Year. There were also fireworks let off whenever they celebrated birthdays.

It took me a long time to twig that the nights when I was highly anxious coincided with those times. Our bathroom had a flat roof and a skylight. It made the room lovely and airy, but it let in noises when I was in the bath. This included the bangers and rockets. My heart would race and not stop until days later. I couldn't settle. I felt the need to get away, fast. I was so confused. What on earth was happening? And why was I seeing dead people?

Several years later, our neighbour started building his own extension. There would be hammer-blows all day, from around nine in the morning through to eight at night. I couldn't concentrate on writing the articles and opinion pieces I loved to write for nursing magazines.

I couldn't settle to watch telly. I would sweat, have a racing heart and anxiety laid heavy on my chest. I couldn't explain this either.

I dearly wished my nursing tutors would have given us time on the psychiatric wards. I'd have understood about PTSD and got treatment earlier. I was a general nurse, and the psychiatric block was spent on a medical and surgical ward and then an isolation unit learning about the psychiatric needs of a general ward patient. Though this was invaluable, I never learned about Post Traumatic Stress Disorder while an army nurse, though I daresay the psychiatric ward must have had several patients being treated for it.

Like most veterans, I loathe bonfire night and Hogmanay. Not because I'm antisocial, (though I am!), but because of the loud noises. I've not been in combat, but that Tornado jet, travelling at some speed, made a loud explosion when it crashed. It must be imprinted on my brain. Similarly, other veterans will have sharp reminders from the retorts of bangers and other fireworks.

My coping strategies is to close all the air vents in the house windows, put on my noise-cancelling headphones and to stay indoors for the nights building up to Bonfire Night and on the 5th of November itself. I don't go to any displays and stay home. I also don't let Lynne out to the garden after five at night. She doesn't like the loud noises either. I give her a lick mat with cream cheese or dog peanut butter spread around it. This distracts her and the licking releases her endorphins, her happy chemicals.

I do the same for Hogmanay. Several minutes to midnight will see me pressing the noise-cancelling button on the side of my headphones and I'll listen to a radio play or music until the noises have settled.

If there is a wedding at the local hotel, I'll get notification of fireworks releases via their Facebook page. They are usually good at announcing the time of their fireworks display for the party there.

Consider how fireworks affect you and what coping strategies you could do to have a safer night when they light up your skies.

CHAPTER 56:

MEDIATION

Relationships will sadly break down when people don't understand PTSD and grief. Other times, people have too much of an understanding and will exploit your suffering for their own nefarious needs. In either case, a professional mediator may be needed.

Some mediation services are free. For example, a local council could introduce an independent mediator to help resolve a dispute between two neighbours. The courts may also use the services of a mediator, perhaps in a dispute between separated couples. Family courts can also use their services to ensure the welfare of children.

Mediators are trained to bring separated parties together, in a neutral setting, and allow both parties to talk about their side of the quarrel to resolve disputes.

They will expertly ensure both sides have talked and, most importantly, have listened to the other party.

It's a great way to resolve disputes amicably, providing each side is willing to participate, listen and find mutual ways to go forward. It can heal many a relationship and friendship.

PTSD may make you act out of character, which can affect your family, friends, and neighbours. Grief can do the same thing. If this has affected you, then please seek a local mediator and find a way forward.

CHAPTER 57:

A FRESH START

Sometimes mediation fails, a problem cannot be overcome, or a home may have too many awful memories. In which case, a fresh start is needed.

I've never been able to go back to the flat where Angus took his life. Abigail lives there now and bravely turned it into her own home. She says she feels closer to Angus there.

Our family home has wonderful memories of the children growing up and despite the neighbourhood noises throughout the day and night, we didn't want to move. We overcame them by soundproofing our home and it has had the added advantage of making it more thermal. Our fuel bills have lowered considerably. But not all issues can be overcome.

I think of someone we met at a support group who found their child dead by suicide, most violently, in the family home. Walking past the place the person's child died was a constant reminder and filled the person with tears and deep sorrow. This person was deeply in grief, even years later. Others in the group advised the person to move home and even offered to help with removals and other practicalities. Sadly, the group member would not move, and neither did their stage of grief.

A fresh start may be needed if you cannot cope with the noises around your home or if it is too painful to be in the place where your loved one died. We are all different and react differently. Some, like Abigail, will draw comfort from being in the place where their loved one died, others, like me, will not. There's no shame. Remember, grief and PTSD affect us all in diverse ways.

CHAPTER 58:

DAILY TREAT

I have a new mantra that I adapted from the Bible; I hope God will forgive me. 'Give me this day your daily treat!'

It took me a long time to consider myself worth it. The depths of my grief and PTSD saw my self-esteem plummet. I didn't consider myself worthy of good food, buying and reading a book from my favourite author, reading my beloved Doctor Who magazine, or watching a DVD. But my psychologist, over months, built up my self-esteem and worth. She advised me to reward myself, in a small way, with a daily treat.

For Karla, it is a Tunnock's treat. Snowballs and the caramel wafers are her favourite. For me, it's taking the time to sit out in the garden with Lynne and watch the birds feed from the fat ball holders I have scattered around. I've been able to achieve peace there, from the loud bangs that previously plagued me, by having cameras filming the area. There is a spacious arbour for Lynne to comfortably lie or sit next to me, or on top of me! She has no concept of personal space!

Other days I add in a favourite home-cooked lunch or a sit down in my armchair with that week's issue of 2000AD. More recently, I've taken to re-reading my old Target novelisations of the classic Doctor Who episodes. I know – don't judge me!

A sure sign that I'm well on the road to recovery and living my best life is that I'm reading the recent novels by my two favourite authors, David Morrell, and Gerald Seymour. I'm retaining each page, following the plot, and loving the journey they take me on. Lynne is busy on the floor with her snuffle mat, digging deep with her snout to get those valuable snacks. Life is glorious, simple, but great. Just how I want it now. I hope reading through this book has helped you see this too and that you are living the best way you can.

CHAPTER 59:

BE GRATEFUL FOR SOMETHING EACH DAY

There are a lot of negativities going on in your mind when you suffer from PTSD. You often ruminate about how you could have done something better or how it was your fault. It's the same with grief.

There is a great exercise that only takes seconds, which has been proven to reset your brain into thinking more positively. It's a quick and easy way to get free Cognitive Behavioural Therapy without paying for the CBT bill! Simply think of one thing that you were grateful for that day. It could be something that happened to you, something you saw, or something someone did. You might find it beneficial to write it down in a notebook that you can look back in.

Here are some examples from my life:

I heard a robin proudly singing in the garden.

Lynne and I sat on our favourite public bench that overlooks the coastline and had a cuddle.

Abigail brought round a surprise Chinese meal.

I could write two-thousand words of my latest novel and introduce a fun, new character.

I baked a loaf in the bread-maker, and it came out perfect.

I met a friend at the Post Office and enjoyed a brief chat.

I watched an episode of 'Allo 'Allo and laughed out loud.

I taught Lynne a new command, and she has mastered it. (This was the drop command – useful for when she returns with a dead rabbit in her mouth!)

I listened to a Chas n' Dave CD – Stop judging me, dear reader!

Try it for at least a week. I'd love to hear your examples. Be warned, it gets addictive! You should soon see life that bit brighter.

CHAPTER 60:

EXERCISE

If you are well enough to do this, then I wholeheartedly recommend taking up one or several forms of exercise. I wrote earlier about the natural happy chemicals that Lynne releases during licking her lick mat. They are also released when she gnaws on her bones or buffalo horn. I wouldn't advocate you try this to release your endorphins! Though, each to their own.

Instead, hit the gym, take up running or swimming, get on your bike, or join a five-a-side team. Do anything that gets your heart rate high. Even gardening is a great exercise. Try to do your exercise outdoors if you can. Get away from your home and smell that sweet fresh air.

You may need to phase things in, so don't sign up for a marathon at the weekend. Take time out to exercise and get those endorphins pumping around your body. Your mind will thank you and you'll notice how much better you feel about yourself and your situation. The adage, 'Healthy body equals healthy mind,' rings true.

I neglected this aspect of my health and became a couch potato. My younger self would have been appalled at the extra four inches I grew around my waist and the three stones I put on during my apathy years. I've lost them, but it was hard work shedding them, especially as I can't exercise because of my dodgy knees. But I could continue with the stretching exercises a physiotherapist taught me. These help support the muscles and tendons around the knees and keeps me on my feet. I do light gardening and go for gentle walks with Lynne. Do what is right for you and enjoy it. Gyms and swimming pools can be social places to meet up with friends or find new pals. Embrace this life.

Find the sport or exercise that you like and build up the time you do it and the effort involved. Learn to love those endorphins.

CHAPTER 61:

WALKING

Walking may be a gentler form of exercise for those of us of a certain age. It'll put less strain on bones. It gets you out and about and provides the ideal time for mindfulness exercises.

Try feeling a tree, relishing the texture of the bark, and smelling the freshness of the air mixed with surrounding grass and flowers. Look at the beauty around you and taste how crisp your breath feels as you slowly inhale through your nostrils and exhale even slower through your mouth. Consider the contrast between your pumping heartbeat from the exercise through to the gradual slowing as you stop to rest and admire the scenery. Listen to the sway of the branches and leaves.

If tree hugging isn't your thing, then go for a coastal walk. Take off your socks and shoes and enjoy the feeling of the wet sand squelching between your toes. Appreciate the gritty texture. Pick up some dry sand as you make your way from the shore and allow it to trickle through your hands. Peer closely and see if you can watch the moments when each grain leaves your fingers and falls to the ground. As you do your breathing exercises, lick your lips, and taste the salty tang. Hear the birds and the gentle lap of the ocean. Try to distinguish each separate bird.

You get the idea. It's all about finding that balance of exercise and connecting with nature. Mindfulness moments are free and are all around us.

You could meet up with a walking partner and explore areas together. The most liberating of chats can be outdoors whilst walking the hills, footpaths, and beaches. That's why so many men chat groups have sprung up around the country. Request to join your local one.

Offer to take a neighbour's dog out if you don't have your own. I guarantee it is splendid company.

Stop reading this and go for a walk!

CHAPTER 62:

PETS

Pets have a peaceful and calming influence on us. Most pets, except for fish, can be stroked and this contact with another being slows our heart rate and breathing and can lower blood pressure. It's been clinically proven that dog owners live longer. I would encourage everyone to own a dog, especially those living with PTSD and grief. Lynne truly has been the major contributor to my improved mental health and is helping me live a healthier lifestyle. I'm too busy feeding her instead of feeding myself all the wrong things. I use positive training to teach her new things every day and she responds well to treats. Though I do have to watch my fingers. She's like Arkwright's old till in Open All Hours!

I go for a daily stroll with her, usually to places she can run free and burn off her energy. She gets me out of the house and gives me the confidence to go places like shops and even the cinema. Otherwise, I'd just stay at home, eating all the wrong snacks, feeling morose, dwelling on things I should leave in the past.

Grooming her is therapeutic, as I love the softness of her coat, especially after a brush. It's like warm silk. She loves a good tummy rub afterwards.

I call her my miracle dog. Karla calls her something else!

I used to keep chickens and even they were great fun and got me in the garden to feed them, let them run around and ensure their safety. They are surprisingly warm, and their feathers are so soft and mine used to enjoy sitting on my lap and having a few strokes. Each had their own personalities. I miss their tasty fresh eggs, especially the double-yolks.

My fantail white doves are fun to watch. I love the way their heads bob and they look magnificent when flying around the rooftops. They cleverly group together and fly in formation. Their cooing is so rhythmically calming. I can never tire of watching them plop into the sputnik trap and make their way safely into the shed. Their plumage keeps brilliantly white, and it's a joy to watch them have a bath and preen themselves. When it rains, they go into the aviary and spread one wing wide to have a free shower, then it folds cleverly back to their body, and they spread their other wing out and repeat the process.

Karla has a tortoise. He doesn't do much, (a bit like Karla!), but he does like to waddle around the house and enjoy a salad feast in his vivarium. By the way, my cheek is suddenly sore and red. I don't think my wife liked that comment!

Abigail has a rabbit and two gerbils and loves to have them hopping around her flat and running around her lap. She's also got an aquarium and finds pleasure in stocking it with colourful fish and finds peace in watching them dart about.

Consider getting a pet. Caring for it will be a beneficial distraction from all the stress in your life.

CHAPTER 63:

BURP BURPS!

I knew this chapter heading would grab your attention. Lady of the House Lynne loves her routines. It provides stability and reassurance. Straight after eating her evening meal, she loves to come running through to me, jumps up and places her front paws around my neck and then belches. I get a face full of chewed bran flakes. Ever since, I rub her belly, pat it, and say, 'Burp, burp, burp.' I always get rewarded with another belch and some more bran flakes. She eats these to stop her anal glands getting compacted. They are mixed in with her kibbles and some chopped carrot. Then I ask her if she wants to go outside for, 'Wee wees?' That's her cue to snuggle into my neck and we enjoy an embrace whilst Karla tuts and rolls her eyes. We do this every day without fail. It's created a bond between us that can't be broken and helped settle her into her forever home.

 Lynne has other routines, like her go find it games or when she enters the room where Karla is I announce her with a gleeful, 'Here's Lynniepops!'

Karla's routine is to tut and roll her eyes in exasperation. My routine is to ignore her and have fun with Lynne.

There were plenty or routines in nursing. I guess you could call them rituals. They spill over into my personal life and there is one that I am minded about as I write this chapter. But it is one ritual that I pray I never have to do again. The first time I entered Angus's flat after he took his life there, I desperately needed to do something I've done countless times after performing the ritual of last offices as a nurse. This involved washing the body of a recently deceased patient and dressing him or her in a shroud. Either before, or straight after, I would open the window. It was a superstition handed down by other nurses and taught by my nursing tutors that this released the soul. Some nurses believed it would stop the ghost of the patient haunting the hospital, hospice, or nursing home. Though the body of Angus was no longer there, I needed to believe that his soul could still be released on its journey to heaven. It wasn't rational nor based on science – it was simply a remnant of routine from my ingrained nursing practices. I hope it set him free.

I hope you can see where this is going. Yup, I think routines will benefit you. Going to bed at the same time helps the natural rhythms of your body, the circadian rhythms, keep track and will be conducive to a better sleep. As will getting out of bed at the same time.

Eating regular meals will help with your blood sugars and digestion, especially if you don't have someone to do burp burps with!

Regular exercise will keep you fit and help with your mental health.

All aspects of your daily life could benefit from routines to give you focus and drive.

But don't become a fanatic. Allow room for a break in routine, such as going out for lunch or dinner, or having a lie-in after a rough night's sleep.

CHAPTER 64:

LOCKDOWN

The 2020 Lockdown was a tough time for some people and the Covid pandemic was simply awful. I hope you weren't affected, and your loved ones stayed safe.

For me and Lynne, it proved an unexpected blessing. It allowed everything to slow down, and I gained comfort from being at home, wearing my headphones and not being dragged shopping or to the cinema. We'd never done online grocery or home delivery shopping before, but we were forced to because Karla was on the shielding list. I wish we'd done it sooner. It's so easy and removed a lot of my stress. I hate being trapped in queues and the added stimuli of beeps, alarms, loud music, strangers and having to unpack the trolley and try to pack while holding Lynne's leash, while trying to stop strangers stroking her and distracting her, feeding her, clucking at her from across the aisles, paying the bill, pushing the trolley, and getting Lynne to refocus on me and not people petting her. It blew my mind!

But home shopping could be done from my armchair. We could plan our meals and not be tempted into impulse purchases of sugary food. We could stay in budget too. The doorstep delivery takes seconds to bring into my house. It's marvellous!

The other benefit of Lockdown was not going to the cinema each week to see several films in one day. It's surprising how often a helicopter will suddenly appear, looming large and with stereo sound of rotors playing around the room, a room that I may be trapped in because of people on either side of me and, worse of all, behind me. Even the sweetest of romances can have choppers in them. There's a reason I love Westerns and old musicals. Cowboys and Fred Astaire rarely hop on a helicopter.

People stayed away from me during Covid, and I relished having my personal space again. I hate being hugged; it makes me feel trapped, especially by those tight cuddlers. Folk stopped petting Lynne as they tried to social distance and didn't want to be near me in case I was a carrier of the disease. It was the best time ever!

Being forced to stay at home, except for our daily stroll, allowed Lynne and I to bond further. Her focus was purely on me, and we trained hard. I practiced her leave command several times a day by dropping enticing treats on the floor, commanding her to leave it alone. We drilled through her walk to heel by using the 1,2,3 and feed exercise where I say the numbers aloud and on three; she gets a treat. I allowed her to run free on the nearby hills and playing field, then got a strong recall by counting out to ten and then feeding her ten treats, counting each one out, upon her return. Now she comes back when she hears me say one.

The most surprising beneficial aspect for me was when Karla was admitted to hospital. This was a worrying time. Only one visitor could see her, and the rules stipulated it must be the same person for the duration of the hospital admission. We elected it to be Abigail, so she would not worry about her mother if she saw her each day. Then the visiting rules changed, and none were permitted. It was a tough time. It's no wonder my anxiety levels went through the roof when you factor in the risk of Karla contracting Covid in a busy hospital.

Up till then Lynne and I would rarely sleep in the same room, usually only when we stayed overnight in a hotel near Bravehound HQ. On those rare occasions, she would wake me up from my nightmares by nuzzling into me or sharing her tongue with me. Gawds! During Karla's hospital admission, I took Lynne upstairs with me, and she ignored her bed on the floor and slept by me on the bed and a remarkable thing happened. My nightmares lessened. I could go through the night without being in its clutches all-night long. I felt refreshed and clear-headed the next day, so much so that I could spend all day in the study, crafting a new novel.

Lynne would alternate between sleeping with her head on Karla's pillow, facing me, to spooning me, through to sleeping at my feet – all depending on the levels of my anxiety and nightmares.

Karla was not best pleased when she came home! She calls Lynne, 'The Mistress,' and thought that her place had been usurped. But I persisted and Lynne sleeps between us, watching over me, chasing away my nightmares.

Earlier I talked about routines. Lynne and I have a bedtime routine. Karla goes to bed early and Lynne and I join her a few hours later. She jumps up to my side of the bed and waits for me to get undressed, then I give her a nightly biscuit while I jump between the duvet and sheet and race Lynne to my pillow. She always wins and I get a face full of biscuit crumbs as she gives me a kiss, then we cuddle until I fall asleep and she goes and gets comfy, depending on the level of my nightmares. I usually wake up, balancing precariously on the edge of the bed, whilst Lady of the House Lynne is sprawled wide across the duvet. She opens one eye furtively as I dress, and she'll only stir when I open the door. Then she sits on the edge of the bed and has a morning cuddle, then races me down the stairs with her legs going faster than the rest of her. It works for us both and meanwhile, Karla tuts, rolls her eyes, and goes back to sleep!

Friends are aghast and think it unhygienic to sleep with a dog and my younger self would have been surprised at what my sleeping habit is now. But I think my doggie-friendly pals will understand it. Besides, who cares! I detest those nightmares and being anxiety-ridden and will continue this way of living.

I won't end this chapter with my thoughts to you because I hope there will never be another pandemic in our lifetime. Though I would encourage you to have an annual flu vaccination. Grief and PTSD may have lowered your natural immunity.

CHAPTER 65:

CHRISTMAS, BIRTHDAYS AND ANNIVERSARIES

These dates have significant meanings to us all and are the most difficult when we no longer have a loved one there to share them with. The date of Angus's death is etched into my memory and each time it passes, it rips out my heart. I also know the anniversary of the most violent of deaths I've been involved in.

I dread their arrivals. I can't focus, so shelve any work, if I can. I take time to spend these dates with Abigail and Karla and we visit Angus's grave together. We lay flowers, cut from the garden, so he has something from home. Then we go for a meal together.

At Christmas, Karla makes a wreath from the holly in our garden, which is resplendent with bright red berries. She adds decorative ribbons. We go on Christmas Day as a family to spend time at his resting place.

On the day that would have been his birthday, we go to his graveside. It felt odd the year when Abigail surpassed the age of Angus when he died.

When Mother's Day comes, I give Karla extra hugs. I notice she does the same for me at Father's Day. She always makes me a card from Lynne!

On Remembrance Day, we leave our poppies by his headstone.

These rituals are important to us. Angus is still a part of our family.

On the anniversary of the Tornado crash, I have learnt to self-care and take to the nearby hills with Lynne for some solitude and reflection on a job I did to the best of my ability. I do my breathing exercises and meditate. I cuddle Lynne tight. She doesn't leave my side. I guess she knows when I'm not at my best. She's a clever lass and great comfort. My flashbacks are worse on this date.

Such dates will be tough for you as well. Be kind to yourself and put yourself first. Go gently into significant days. Share the relevance of these dates with your pals. If you can, meet up with your other surviving comrades and toast the fallen. Embrace the memories of those you have lost or have been involved in caring for in death.

You will have setbacks as you learn to live with PTSD and grief. Don't beat yourself up. Remind yourself that you are only human. You wouldn't be 'normal' if you didn't have these feelings and setbacks. Just reset yourself. Follow the coping strategies in this book to get you back to the best you can be.

It is said that the first anniversary of a death is the hardest. This is true, but so is the second, the third, and so on. Grief will never leave you. A life can be built around it, but it remains, ready to catch you unawares. Friends and family are great at rallying around you for the first months after a death, but this support may wane as the years go by. They may think you have 'moved on.' But for you and certainly me, the death, and feelings around it, lingers. I don't mind; I want to remember Angus and even seven years after his death, my thoughts are never far from him.

I'll leave this chapter by repeating myself. Be kind to yourself on these dates. Go gently on the build-up and on the day itself.

CHAPTER 66:

STILL
LEARNING/RUMINATING

Being back in the fellowship of veterans provides laughter and friendship. It brings fun back into your life. It is also an opportunity to learn. Despite years of therapy and writing this book, I can still learn valuable lessons and I'd encourage you to keep learning as well.

I was chatting to a former regimental sergeant major and colonel about their PTSD, proof that even top ranks do not escape this condition. Both talked about how they would fret about the least little thing and it would tie them up in knots, mentally, for days, sometimes weeks. This sounded familiar! All three of us agreed dark thoughts would enter, take root, and grow. With it comes anxiety, sleeplessness, and dread. Curses! I thought I was handling this condition well.

As an example. I was in a supermarket, with Lynne by my feet. I was reaching for a carton of milk while talking to Karla. An elderly lady came right behind me unexpectedly and started calling to Lynne, distracting her from her duty. Lynne tugged on the leash, causing me to twist around while making sure I didn't drop her leash or the milk. I totally lost my train of thought with Karla and the inevitable happened – I lost my temper and told the woman off for distracting my assistance dog. The lady, understandably, got upset. I refused to allow her to have a stroke of Lynne and told her she should not distract an assistance dog, as they were there for the benefit of the owner and performing important duties. She apologised and said she didn't know. I went thermonuclear and walked off, leaving poor Karla trailing in my wake. It took me a while to calm down and the shopping trip became a bit of a disaster. Worst still, I ruminated for days about how I'd upset an elderly lady, lost my temper, and forgot to buy items of groceries. I fretted about how I could have handled the situation better without upsetting someone who saw a beautiful dog and wanted to stroke it. My rational mind eventually won the wrestling bout. The woman should not have approached from right behind me. Nor should she have interrupted my conversation with Karla, and she should not have called to Lynne and distracted her from her duty of keeping me calm and confident to be out and about.

I often ruminate about the past. Did I do enough for my patients? Was I a good enough nurse? Is it my fault my parents have ostracised me? Was I a good dad to Angus and Abigail? Am I worthy of Karla's love? Do I deserve to have Lynne in my life? I do battle with these and more – I eventually win. But it has taken me years to get war ready.

Allow your ruminating thoughts in, but don't allow them to conquer. Permit your rational mind in. Talk with those dearest to you about day-to-day ruminating. If you find your thinking gets too darkly intrusive, then seek professional help as soon as you are able.

I'm still learning from others and have learnt to take advice and help from as many sources as possible. I've had to learn to be receptive to such offers. One came from Help for Heroes. My trusty headphones, after five years of faithful service, were coming to the end of their life. I couldn't afford another pair, so approached Help for Heroes. They generously funded me another top of the range pair so that I don't hear distressing noises like helicopter rotor blades and loud bangs.

The assessor also suggested I attend weekly counselling for free through Hidden Wounds. I thought I'd had plenty of counselling and had no unresolved issues. How wrong was I! The counsellor gave me extra sessions as I had a lot to unpack. Who knew – certainly not me and my denial! We explored the trauma of my service life, Angus's suicide, my childhood, living with PTSD and new coping strategies. I liked the way she described it as having a box or a toolkit where I could go and remove things to help me cope. In it I put Breakaway biscuits, my Nana's favourite treat. I eat these slowly when things get too bad for me and remember the comfort of being with her. It's a sugary treat I make an exception for these days. I carry the Lux scented handkerchief everywhere I go. I do the breathing exercises each day, sometimes several times a day, and repeat a mantra of 'Calm' with each inhalation and 'Peace' with each exhalation. It's a new technique the Hidden Wounds counsellors taught me to lower my racing mind and heart rate. Other times I need to do them ten or twenty times in a day. The counsellor acknowledged the substantial support I receive from Bravehound and having Lynne and encouraged me to continue to cuddle her and have daily walks. Best of all, she reinforced my belief that I am so happy in Lynne's company and the simple life we lead.

CHAPTER 67:

MY FUTURE

It's been therapeutic writing about my life, my PTSD and grief. I've learnt a lot about myself. I can see how far I'm come in the last dreadful six years. Looking back, I can see how ill I was and how close to death I've been. Fiona, the founder of Bravehound, reminded me recently that when I first came to the HQ I could not face eating in a crowded hall with the other veterans and had my first meal there in a room with just Karla. Then I slowly progressed to sitting at the long table and gradually interacting with others. Now I enjoy the company of the other veterans and their dogs and look forward to going to Bravehound events.

Most of all, I see the kindness of Abigail, Karla, our friends, and strangers who have helped us get back on our feet and cope with a life without Angus. The various military and grief charities have shown us that Angels walk this earth. Without their support, I doubt I'd be alive. Without my Lynniepops, I would not be here to type away. She's currently crunching down on an oesophagus – Gawds! But a big yum yums from her!

I don't make long-term plans. I love my writing and concentrate on that. It keeps my mind away from other thoughts. I enter each book into a literary competition, and it would be a great help if you left a review at Amazon. The judges look at the number of reviews and ratings. Just a sentence or two if you enjoyed a novel of mine, or how this self-help autobiography book has helped you. Thanks!

Every day, without fail, I do my calming exercises. I take my medicines and my wonderful doctor checks in with me regularly. She keeps me at my healthiest and I love her no-nonsense approach. She says what needs saying. I'm trying to lose a few more pounds. But I still treat myself. Last evening, I enjoyed a kafir with a chopped banana and a handful of crushed walnuts and cashew nuts. This yoghurt helps my gastric problems, but that'll be the only sugar I eat all week. Then it's straight back to my low-fat, high-protein, plant-based diet. I'm back to the weight and waist size I was when Angus died.

Lynne and I go out at least five days a week for a gentle walk.

I keep Angus in my heart and honour the deaths I've been involved with and keep them at bay with Lynne's help.

I find humour in running Lynne's social media accounts and love interacting with her followers. She's just joined TikTok! But my favourite account is on Twitter @lyn_golden where I love seeing photos of her doggie friends. Some comments make me laugh out loud.

We continue with the scent work training, and I look forward to going to Bravehound HQ and seeing the mascot, sweet Gwyneth. Fiona, the founder of Bravehound, is a pleasure to be around. As are the trainers, like Kerry and Al, and volunteers like Pamela and Hugh. Fiona has a lovely calming manner and her vision for the charity has helped so many veterans. I'm indebted to her and the family who kindly donated Lynne in memory of their wife/mother. They have kept me alive and given me a focus. Most of all, they have brought fun back into the lives of Abigail, Karla, and I. Shhh! Lynne is still the naughtiest Bravehound, but don't tell them!

Though I think this secret is no more because Lynne and I were at Bravehound HQ, doing more scent work training. She was tasked with finding a hidden tin with gun oil. She did ever so well, clearing a six-bed barrack room. Then she repeated the task and was sniffing under a wardrobe and found an old sock. Her arcing tail wagged around and around with glee. She clamped her teeth down tight on this found high-value asset, looked at me and the trainer, Karen, and swallowed it whole. Ooops! I didn't even have time to say the "Drop" command. I had to confess her actions to the Bravehound dog trainers and Fiona, who were in the main meeting room. Then it was off to the vets with Fiona and Lynne. She got a quick injection, Lynne, not Fiona, and then barfed the sock up before it could cause any intestinal damage. She was as good as gold on the drive back. As she didn't seem too bad, I took her back into the main room, which served as the Cadets' adult instructors' Sergeants Mess. Lynne promptly spewed over their immaculate carpet - at the feet of Fiona. I think her naughty secret is no more!

Despite her naughty streak, I would not be without her. My anxiety gets bumped away by Lynne, and my depression is manageable. The fresh air helps, as does getting in touch with nature.

I still go to Thermonuclear level, but the anger has all gone. I simply strip off layers and have a cuddle with my best friend. She soon sees off panic attacks. I'm still working on the imposter syndrome and survivor's guilt, though I have a stern word with myself when this, and dread, tries to creep up on me. The discussions with Hidden Wounds and their professional therapy have helped immensely with these issues.

Lynne is flat out asleep by my feet. The gnawing at the stinky treat has tired her out, so I'll join her in an afternoon nap and get back to you with the last chapter.

CHAPTER 68:

YOUR FUTURE

You have one and deserve one. I hope I've guided you to leading a better life and have given you plenty of coping strategies. A life with PTSD and grief can be rebuilt and reshaped.

I love hearing from readers. If you've been helped by this book or want to suggest other sources of help or coping mechanisms, then get in touch at www.facebook.com/cgbuswell or let me know at www.cgbuswell.com/contact.php and I'll add them to new editions.

You will have setbacks. Don't beat yourself up. Acknowledge your feelings and go back to the coping mechanisms. Learn to live and love again.

Bye for now.

Chris and Lynne.

ACKNOWLEDGEMENTS

My grateful thanks to the author Damien Lewis for his book cover quote. Damien is the Patron of Bravehound, and it means a lot to me that he takes an interest in us recipients. He took the time to read this book and provide a quote for the cover. He writes in-depth and fascinating accounts of Special Forces missions.

www.damienlewis.com

I'm indebted to Fiona at Bravehound in so many ways. Thank you for writing the incredibly moving foreword for the book and setting me on the path to recovery with my beloved Lynne.

www.bravehound.co.uk

As always, my heartfelt gratitude goes to my advanced reader team of my dear friends, Ray and Katherine. Ray is a fountain of knowledge of all things IT and can be found at

www.crudenbaytraining.co.uk

Amanda, at Let's Get Booked, has produced another brilliant cover, and expertly formatted my manuscript. Thank you. Amanda has graciously provided this for free and donated her fee to Bravehound. Thank you so much, Amanda, for your kind generosity. See more of her amazing animal covers at:

www.letsgetbooked.com

Karla, the Other Woman, also proofreads my novels, and, whether I like to admit this – though mostly not, she is my psychological carer. Lynne and I love having you in our lives! Thank you for tolerating The Mistress and me! Karla's stunning portrait painting of Gwyneth, the Bravehound mascot, is on the back cover. Karla specialises in pet portraits and is available for commissions.

The photos of Lynne and me on the front and back cover are by Lauren Norris and more of her work can be seen at

www.facebook.com/LaurenNorrisPhoto

Thank you, Lauren, for the magnificent photographs that capture Lynne's beauty.

OTHER BOOKS I'VE WRITTEN:

The Fence

The infected want to kill him. Jason Harper needs to survive and find his wife. He doesn't trust his companion.

Former Royal Air Force Regiment Gunner Jason Harper witnesses a foreign jet fly over his Aberdeenshire home. It is spilling a strange yellow smoke. Minutes later, his wife, Pippa, telephones him, shouting that she needs him. They then get cut off. He sets straight out, unprepared for the nightmare that unfolds during his journey. Everyone seems to want to kill him.

Along the way, he pairs up with fellow survivor Imogen. But she enjoys killing the living dead far too much. Will she kill Jason in her blood thirst? Or will she hinder his journey through this zombie filled dystopian landscape to find his pregnant wife?

The Fence is the first in this series of post-apocalyptic military survival thrillers from the torturous mind of British horror and science fiction novel writer C.G. Buswell.

Download at https://www.amazon.co.uk/dp/B09ZFB31NY/

One Last War

Think YOU have a nightmare neighbour?

Surely no one's neighbour could be this vindictive over just a few birds?

Former special forces soldier Carl hopes to put his combat days behind him when he moves with his wife and young children to a peaceful Scottish village.

But his nightmare neighbour soon starts a battle of wits with him. Does this SAS Trooper have one more war left in him?

One Last War is an angst-ridden suspenseful novel with a wicked twist from the dark mind of C.G. Buswell

Buy now from www.amazon.co.uk/gp/product/B089WKB13D/

Review

"One Last War is a great read, particularly for a veteran or forces family member. For those with an interest in Post Traumatic Stress Disorder and the role of Assistance dogs, it should be required reading."

Fiona MacDonald Founder and Director of military charity BRAVEHOUND.

Free Novella - Operation Wrath

The death of the Brotherhood will be avenged.

RAF gunner Jason Harper and a team of Special Air Service operators are enraged after the death of their brothers by a terrorist drone strike. They fly into south-eastern Yemen on a Black-op mission to gather intelligence and avenge the death of their comrades.

Can they infiltrate the Al-Queda insurgents' camp, stay undetected, and call down their own drone missile strike and get home safely?

Will they all survive to fight another day?

Operation Wrath is a free, fast-paced adventure prequel to the non-stop action series, The Fence, by military veteran author C.G. Buswell.

Download for free https://dl.bookfunnel.com/ronb0lcogs on any device and read today.

The Grey Lady Ghost of the Cambridge Military Hospital

Corporal Scott Grey is drawn into a never-ending war in the past.

He's a military nurse, desperate to find peace with his fiancé, Naomi, a fellow army medic. But he is haunted by his experiences in Iraq and Afghanistan.

He is still recovering in Aldershot from a serious head injury that affects him physically and emotionally, when one unsettled night a ghost nurse, a Grey Lady, from World War I, takes him back to the horrors of the trenches, and shares her story of loss.

He's not sure if she's real or just a manifestation of the head injury. But when she pulls him back in time to her world, it seems all too real.

221

These time slip experiences recur as the WW1 nurse returns again and again to take Scott through her own tragic story. What does she want from him? And how will this affect Scott's relationship with Naomi in the present day?

Scott wants desperately to stay in his own time and with his fiancé, but the Grey Lady is equally determined to find her lost love, a handsome Gordon Highlander.

Can they both return to their own true loves, or will he be trapped in her world forever on an unending search? Scott's peace and sanity hang in the balance.

Can the two nurses heal each other? One finding peace, the other at last able to rest in peace.

Buy now from www.amazon.co.uk/gp/product/B0151WFH9U/

Printed in Great Britain
by Amazon

26766302R00136